Team Analytics

Written by authors who have real-world experience of leading teams and major projects, this book explores a new approach to project success: the continuous process of enabling and empowering teams to reach the optimal levels of performance. For decades, project managers have been asking the multi-million, and sometimes multi-billion-dollar question: why did the project fail? High project failure rates are nothing new and have been well documented, but when project professionals seek answers, they usually return to the original project plan to identify flaws. Yet there is one place where most don't look for the answers: the people. Here is the value gap of the almost untouched area of project team performance management that has the potential to be the next quantum leap in project success. PMO leaders, change executives, HR professionals, project managers, program managers, and portfolio managers – anyone who leads a team in the project world – will learn how to make this critical investment for any organization which wishes to thrive in the 'new normal' project-based economy.

Bentzy Goldman, founded Perflo, an innovative technology start-up that helps teams and their organizations to measure and increase performance using cutting-edge research in team psychology. He is extremely passionate about and speaks on topics related to the future of work – dreaming of a world where Monday mornings are looked forward to, not resented. You can discover more about Bentzy at www.futureofworkguy.com

Peter Taylor, keynote speaker and coach, is the author of the number 1 bestselling project management book *The Lazy Project Manager*, along with many other books on Project Management. He has built and led some of the largest PMOs in the world with organizations such as Siemens, IBM, UKG, and now Ceridian, where he is the VP Global PMO. He has also delivered over 500 lectures around the world in 25 countries and has been described as 'perhaps the most entertaining and inspiring speaker in the project management world today'. You can discover more about Peter through his website www.thelazyprojectmanager.com

Team Analytics

The Future of High-Performance Teams and Project Success

Bentzy Goldman and Peter Taylor

Routledge
Taylor & Francis Group
NEW YORK AND LONDON

First published 2023
by Routledge
605 Third Avenue, New York, NY 10158

and by Routledge
4 Park Square, Milton Park, Abingdon, Oxon, OX14 4RN

Routledge is an imprint of the Taylor & Francis Group, an informa business

Library of Congress Cataloguing-in-Publication Data
Names: Taylor, Peter, 1957- author. | Goldman, Bentzy, author.
Title: Team analytics : the future of high-performance teams and project success / Peter Taylor, Bentzy Goldman.
Description: New York, NY : Routledge, 2023. | Includes bibliographical references and index.
Identifiers: LCCN 2022039278 (print) | LCCN 2022039279 (ebook) | ISBN 9781032012230 (hardback) | ISBN 9781032012285 (paperback) | ISBN 9781003177753 (ebook)
Subjects: LCSH: Teams in the workplace. | Positive psychology. | Psychology, Industrial. | Corporate culture.
Classification: LCC HD66 .T396 2023 (print) | LCC HD66 (ebook) | DDC 658.4/022--dc23/eng/20221104
LC record available at https://lccn.loc.gov/2022039278
LC ebook record available at https://lccn.loc.gov/2022039279

ISBN: 978-1-032-01223-0 (hbk)
ISBN: 978-1-032-01228-5 (pbk)
ISBN: 978-1-003-17775-3 (ebk)

DOI: 10.4324/9781003177753

Typeset in Bembo
by MPS Limited, Dehradun

Team Analytics

The Future of High-Performance Teams and Project Success

Bentzy Goldman and Peter Taylor

Routledge
Taylor & Francis Group
NEW YORK AND LONDON

First published 2023
by Routledge
605 Third Avenue, New York, NY 10158

and by Routledge
4 Park Square, Milton Park, Abingdon, Oxon, OX14 4RN

Routledge is an imprint of the Taylor & Francis Group, an informa business

Library of Congress Cataloguing-in-Publication Data
Names: Taylor, Peter, 1957- author. | Goldman, Bentzy, author.
Title: Team analytics : the future of high-performance teams and project success / Peter Taylor, Bentzy Goldman.
Description: New York, NY : Routledge, 2023. | Includes bibliographical references and index.
Identifiers: LCCN 2022039278 (print) | LCCN 2022039279 (ebook) | ISBN 9781032012230 (hardback) | ISBN 9781032012285 (paperback) | ISBN 9781003177753 (ebook)
Subjects: LCSH: Teams in the workplace. | Positive psychology. | Psychology, Industrial. | Corporate culture.
Classification: LCC HD66 .T396 2023 (print) | LCC HD66 (ebook) | DDC 658.4/022--dc23/eng/20221104
LC record available at https://lccn.loc.gov/2022039278
LC ebook record available at https://lccn.loc.gov/2022039279

ISBN: 978-1-032-01223-0 (hbk)
ISBN: 978-1-032-01228-5 (pbk)
ISBN: 978-1-003-17775-3 (ebk)

DOI: 10.4324/9781003177753

Typeset in Bembo
by MPS Limited, Dehradun

Bentzy – Dedicated to everyone who helped me build Perflo, especially our A-Team!

Peter – to my amazing team at Ceridian – Go GPMO!

Contents

Foreword x

1 Introduction 1

2 Part 1: Teams 3

3 The history of teams 4

4 The sociology of teams 5

5 The case for teams 6

6 It's not all roses 8

7 Team diversity 9

8 Teams of the future 11

9 The human-centric organization 14

10 Infusing behavioral science into the workplace 18

11 Where does this leave us? 19

12 Team performance 20

13 Servant leadership and team performance 23

14 Sports psychology and team performance 24

15 The secret superpower of team intelligence 29

16 From assumption to data – introducing team analytics 37

17 Leveraging AI for team effectiveness 50

18 Long-term business benefits 53

19 Conclusion 54

20 Part 2: Projects 55

21 Why projects (still) aren't successful 56

22 The missing phase of Tuckman's model of team development 59

23 Why project teams are simply different to other teams 65

24 It's all gone virtual 69

25 Creative teaming, when two different worlds collide 73

26 Why does it even matter? 77

27 The value of positive teams 79

28 People first 82

29 The truth about project team performance 86

30 It is not big brother 88

31 How is intelligence extracted from data? 90

32 Project intelligence 94

33 Part 3: Futures 97

34 Old way – new way thinking 98

35 T.E.A.M 99

36 But this is an HR thing? 100

37 The Goldman-Taylor five principles of progression 101

38 Part 4: Roadmap 104

39 How to go about the transformation 105

40 Gaining the team buy-in 107

41 Dealing with manager accountability 109

42 Securing the all-important sponsorship 110

43 Steps to success 111

44 A helping hand 112

45 Team analytics: The future of high-performance teams and project success 113

Appendices 114
Index 116

Foreword

How many times have you heard leaders say, "It's all about the people"?

The truth is, "It is all about the people and how they work TOGETHER as a team."

The potential impact of a team is far greater than the sum of its parts. This is as true in business as it is in sports. Each team member can learn the plays and understand the overall strategy, but wins are born out of everyone working in concert – creating a flywheel of success for themselves and the business they work for.

Group dynamics are a complicated and powerful thing. They seem like something a team leader should deal with on their own, but in the real world - answers usually come from the team itself. If you think about teams that you've been a part of, disfunctions are clear to all but tend to fester until they become unmanageable. Then finally someone steps up, creates meaningful clarity, and makes all the difference.

In this book, Bentzy outlines an approach to creating that clarity early in the game, not after it's too late. He leverages experiential data focused on collaboration, well-being, trust, and purpose. All of which, we intuitively know to be critical when it comes to team performance. He essentially hands the reader an approach to proactively improve these foundational building blocks of team performance.

And Peter applies this right thinking to the world of project management and change leadership, exploring the unique dynamics of a project team brough together to deliver this temporary endeavour in the most efficient way.

As you embark on this journey to greater project success you will find yourself with a great deal more insight you can act on. The trick will be to review and act on it as a team – owning the issues and defining solutions together.

Team Analytics: The Future of High-Performance Teams and Project Success is your guide on that journey, aiding your understanding of how your team(s) are working together, and how you, as the leader can harness the collective power of the people.

Remember, "It's all about the people, working together as a team."

Dave Garret
Chief Strategy & Growth Officer at
Project Management Institute - Founder of
www.projectmanagement.com

1 Introduction

Bentzy Goldman

As someone who is very analytical, and a bit of a nerd when it comes to human performance, it would make sense that I've built a company in the area of 'Human Analytics'.

This isn't a cold-blooded experiment purely for the pursuit of optimization treating humans as machines (I'm no engineer). This is from the perspective of 'let's use data analytics to humanize the workplace' – helping teams increase their performance – ultimately leads to a better work-life for all, and who would say no to that. I've been obsessed with new and better ways of working, management processes, and the research in psychology from even before I entered the workforce.

A bit of a rebel from the early days, I was what the adults in the room would call a nuisance, but what I humbly thought of as an inquisitive contrarian. Perhaps a bit of both. This inquisitiveness and yearning for change despite decades of stagnation and the all too painful 'this is how we've always done things', drives me to wake up every day and carry the message of change to every organization, manager, and employee out there.

We spend so much of our lives at work, building our careers and knowledge – we may as well enjoy it. I also think it's time to change the word employee, it gives off such a feeling of enslavement but that's another book. I'm both pleased and honored that Peter, a dear advisor to our start-up and a solid guy that wears his heart on his sleeve – invited me to co-author this book. Peter has been instrumental in the development of our product, thought leadership, and my personal development.

Peter Taylor

Having led some of the largest PMOs in the world, with hundreds of project managers and thousands of projects each year, I recognized early on the value gap in the almost untouched area of project team performance management, which I believe will be the next quantum leap in project success.

DOI: 10.4324/9781003177753-1

It is about ensuring greater alignment amongst project team members knowing that projects are about people, and people (teams) deliver project success.

And this is exactly what led me to say a very swift 'Yes' when Bentzy came a calling a few years back with his ambition in the arena of 'Human Analytics'.

I have said it many, many times over the years – projects are about people. End.

And the people leaders need some help to get the most out of their teams and to support the team member's needs, today and tomorrow.

When I started in project management, I really had no idea about the 'mechanics' of project management but I guess I did have an affinity for people and how to connect them with a common purpose.

I am therefore more than delighted to now have this opportunity to write a book with my friend and business partner, Bentzy, exploring this amazing world of people and how they can achieve so many astonishing things in life through collaborative teamwork.

The book

We know that throughout any project lifecycle there are a plethora of issues that can arise which can threaten the project success. These issues creep up on project managers despite the risk management performed and forecasts put in place, project leaders are constantly investigating where things went wrong analyzing why they did and strategizing how they can be avoided in the future.

Of course, when these exercises are done the answers are not always found and if they ever are, it's all but too late. This breeds the need for a fresh approach to project performance, an approach that seeks to understand first and foremost, those that execute and receive the project plan, the people. This approach should be a holistic one where all likelihoods are evaluated, and bias is removed, and it should be proactive and less reactive, less periodical, and more real time.

In this book, we will explore this new approach to project success, the continuous process of enabling and empowering teams to reach the optimal levels of performance.

2 Part 1: Teams

In Part 1 Bentzy Goldman considers the future of work itself, how it relates to teams, and discovers the true insight into what makes a team a high-performance team (to which we all want to reach), whilst looking 'under the cover' at the intelligence of team analytics to power such high-performance aspirations.

DOI: 10.4324/9781003177753-2

3 The history of teams

Psychological research on the nature of work groups dates back at least to the Hawthorne studies of the 1920s and 1930s,[1,2] they were not however referred to as teams yet. The study concluded amongst other things – that positive human connection among workers did correlate to increased productivity. Who would've thought? By the 1950s when frameworks such as performance appraisals began to take shape,[3] research into how humans at work can be most productive, soared. The nature of topics addressing work groups, i.e., teams, has since expanded significantly.

We know that as factory jobs became more and more automated, there was less of a need for individual workers to perform redundant tasks on their own. We've now gone through a few versions of the 'industrial revolution',[4] to the point where in most scenarios, working in anything but a team makes little sense.

Unfortunately, however many organizations still approach the employee/work experience from a very individualistic mindset however. Take performance management for example, where employees are ranked and stacked against each other to arrive at a score for each employee. Luckily most organizations are evolving with the research, and with the advancements in collaboration tools, and new ways of working – we are making progress, despite it taking almost a century in this specific area.

However, there is still a large disconnect between what the research says and how we work. As we will explore in this book, when you approach team performance from a scientific perspective, and apply these learnings in a humanistic fashion, the results are not only evident, but astounding. I believe it is critical for leaders to understand the evolution of teams and stay abreast of the latest research, to advance and apply our knowledge to achieve optimal team formation, performance, and satisfaction.

Notes

1 "The Hawthorne Effect and Behavioral Studies – Verywell Mind." https://www.verywellmind.com/what-is-the-hawthorne-effect-2795234
2 https://www.oxfordreference.com/view/10.1093/oi/authority.20111110182001101
3 A Brief History of Performance Management - People HR
4 Industrial Revolution – Wikipedia https://en.wikipedia.org/wiki/Industrial

DOI: 10.4324/9781003177753-3

4 The sociology of teams

Although we are quite ahead in our shift from 'individual to team' in the workplace, and despite the many different advancements in team-collaboration methods and technology – there is still a disconnect. We are all still, at our core, driven by the same primal human instincts, and little has changed fundamentally since the days of our evolutionary ancestors, who also had to form teams and work interdependently through challenges. Challenges arguably far greater than an IT implementation (although some would contest this).

The evidence-based ideas of belongingness, social exclusion, human grouping etc., all present a powerful case for team-based models of working, beyond simply the productivity benefits. Our insatiable desire as homo-sapiens to form connections with those around us and create community in which to co-exist and thrive does not subside as soon as we walk through office sliding doors. Studies have proven that social relationships are a greater cause of happiness than money and material objects. Today more than ever the need for belonging has increased dramatically despite the hundreds of social media applications that are supposedly built to 'connect us'. Loneliness has been proclaimed an actual epidemic by medical associations across America, as it has severe mental and emotional health consequences – social isolation being a major risk factor for suicide deaths.

I speak to these tragedies in the hopes that leaders become more aware of the immense importance of building and sustaining healthy teams within their organizations. It could literally save lives. Since the COVID-19 pandemic, the rates of loneliness, alongside the need for belonging, have increased dramatically. Never before has there been a more important time to be purposeful and intentional about how we think of team structures and team empowerment within our organizations. Aside from the many benefits team-based working brings, teams can provide support and encouragement, offering emotional and social support to members, which also leads to increased job satisfaction, engagement, and of course employee retention.

DOI: 10.4324/9781003177753-4

5 The case for teams

Generally, when it comes to knowledge work - teams are more effective than individuals working alone. It's already been proven,[1] but in case you're still skeptical, I will add a bit of stats to the mix.

In the most overly simplistic explanation you'll ever hear about the benefits of teams over individuals: When you have a team of people working together, you can get more done in less time. Teams can divvy up the work and each person can focus on their strengths. This division of labor makes it possible to get more done in less time. Teams also allow for more creativity and collaboration – they can bounce ideas off each other and come up with creative solutions to problems. This collaborative approach leads to better results than if each person was working alone. Below are some high-level benefits of team-based working.

Why teams are more effective than individuals

Three critical arguments for the power of teams[2]:

- Teams allow for division of labor: each person can focus on their strengths and the team can get more done in less time.
- Teams lead to more creativity and collaboration: teams can bounce ideas off each other and come up with creative solutions to problems.
- Teams provide support and encouragement to each other, leading to a higher engaged and productive workforce (Figure 5.1).

The power of teams

- Teams are more likely to achieve larger goals than individuals alone
- Teams are more likely to come up with innovative ideas than individuals
- Teams have been shown to be more productive than individual workers by specifically on tasks that require:

DOI: 10.4324/9781003177753-5

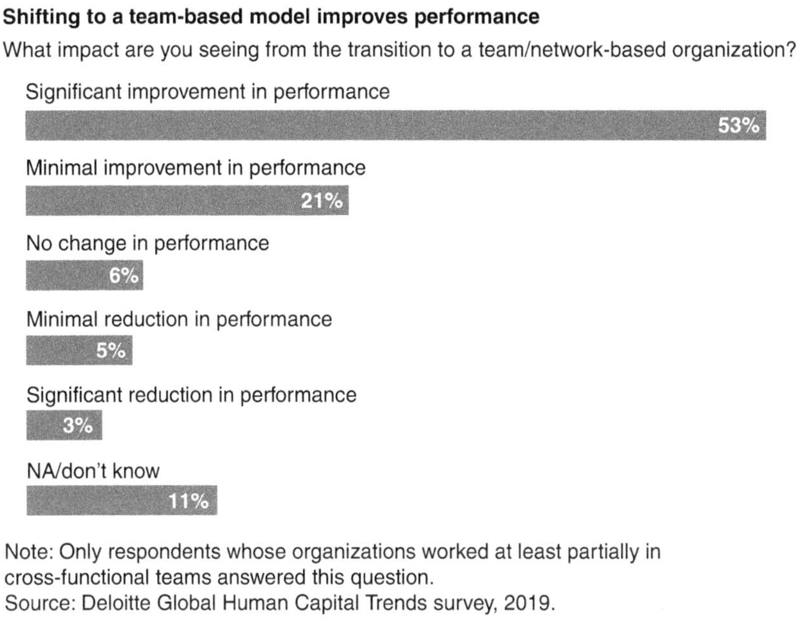

Figure 5.1 Shifting to a team-based model. (Credit; Deloitte).

    - brainstorming
    - problem-solving
    - creativity

- Teams can also help businesses to adapt to change faster: teams are flexible and can quickly adapt to changes in the marketplace or workplace.

The advantages of teams over individual workers are clear. Teams are more productive, creative, and adaptive than individuals.

But aside from just the productivity and innovation benefits of team-based working. Teams allow businesses to tap into a larger pool of talent: by forming teams, businesses can draw on the strengths of a wider range of employees, demographics, and cultures.

Notes

1 https://psycnet.apa.org/record/2017–04389-001
2 https://www.apa.org/news/press/releases/2006/04/group
https://www.forbes.com/2010/08/05/teams-teamwork-individuals-leadership-managing-collaboration.html?sh=42e66c2d5e86
https://study.com/academy/lesson/why-teams-are-more-effective-than-groups.html
Creativity in Teams - Thompson - - Major Reference Works - Wiley Online ...

6 It's not all roses

Of course, many challenges come with teams, from the very beginning of who to put on a team, to the conflict that can arise during their time together, and of course to the misalignment and confusion due to things like the broken telephone.

Building and leading a solid team takes an incredible amount of purposefulness and constant attention to ensure people are working together in harmony toward a common objective that is understood clearly by all. Many challenges can and will arise during a team's time together, whether it may stem from cultural or personal clashes, or perhaps one team member is riding on the work of the rest, causing frustration. They will happen, and we need to be prepared for dealing with these situations.

Yes, putting effort into forming a team based on skills and personalities could help, but things change, people's true selves emerge, or the stress just brings out the worst version of themselves. What many people get wrong is, thinking that the composition of a team is the answer to building an all-star team, when the research (and first-hand experience) proves that no matter the quality of team members, the emergence of behaviors within the team, their unique dynamics, and their eventual collaboration style– are more determining factors in the team's success.

It's also considerably more challenging to get right when team members collaborate virtually with little to no in-person interaction – which is why it's even more crucial to be super purposeful and monitor team dynamics continuously. It should be the utmost priority of team-driven organizations, to equip team leaders and members with the training and support to continuously develop and work through these challenges together.

It's the resilient teams that outperform the rest during times of change, and without a leader to inspire that resilience – team members become unmotivated and check out.

DOI: 10.4324/9781003177753-6

7 Team diversity

Research shows that diverse teams are more successful and innovative.[1] Diversity in teams can mean different things: demographic diversity (race, gender, age, etc.), cognitive diversity (different ways of thinking), and experiential diversity (different experiences and perspectives). Teams that are diverse in all three of these areas are more likely to be successful than teams that lack diversity.

Diversity is critical for teams because it allows teams to: draw on a wider range of skills, knowledge, and perspectives – generating more creative solutions, and catering for the many variables that go into a decision. In order for teams to be diverse it is important for organizations to encourage diversity in the composition of teams as well facilitate a culture of inclusive collaborating.

The good news is, with the rise of virtual work, and organizations hiring talent in different countries, teams will naturally become more diverse, creating new innovations and better ideas. So, as teams become more diverse, they will be better equipped to meet the needs of the modern workplace.

Executive teams have the advantage of being able to make decisions quickly. However, these teams may lack the diversity of skills and knowledge of larger teams. The need for diversity in executive teams is evident as are the benefits of executive team diversity.

McKinsey found that companies with more diverse leadership are better at winning top talent,[2] improving employee satisfaction and decision-making – leading to a virtuous cycle of positive returns. They also suggest that diversity in other areas such as age and experience is likely to bring a competitive advantage for companies that continue attracting and retaining diverse talent (Figures 7.1 and 7.2).

DOI: 10.4324/9781003177753-7

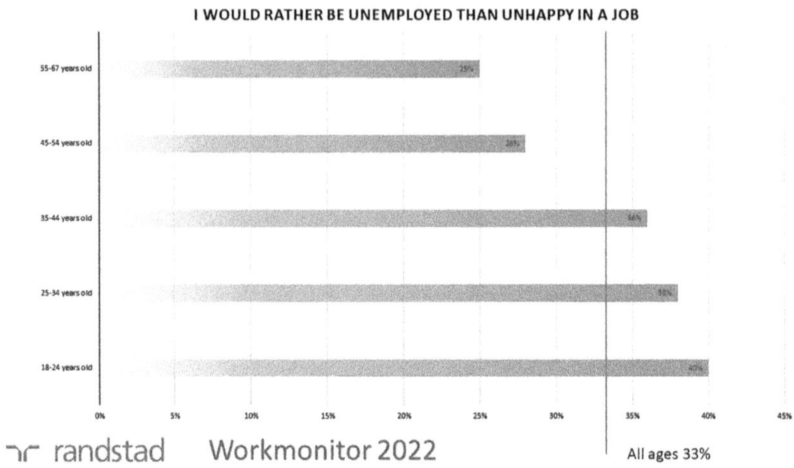

Figure 7.1 Workmonitor 2022 – happiness.

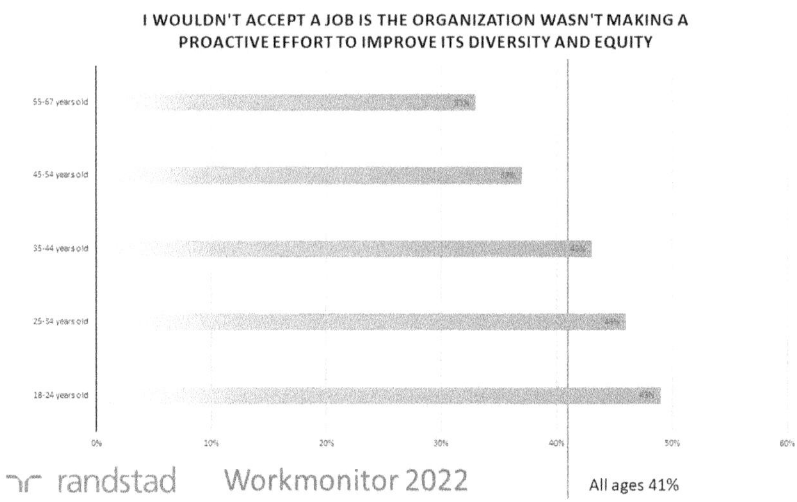

Figure 7.2 Workmonitor 2022 – dei.

Notes

1 How Diversity Makes Teams More Innovative - Strategic Leadership.
2 Diversity wins: How inclusion matters - McKinsey & Company.

8 Teams of the future

As we evolve as humans, and as society progresses both culturally and technologically – so too our model of what a team is and how it should operate needs to evolve. Until now there have been standard types of teams built for different purposes.

Teams evolve

Teams can be formed to complete a once-off project, to develop a new product or service, to test and improve the quality of those products, or they can even exist to solely serve other teams. Teams can also be temporary or permanent, and they can be small or large. The size and composition of the team will depend on the task at hand. Each type of team has its own advantages and disadvantages. Project teams have the advantage of being able to focus all of their energy on the task at hand. However, they may lack the continuity and cohesion of permanent teams.

Product development teams are responsible for developing new products or services. These teams typically consist of experts from different areas such as marketing, engineering, and design. Product development teams have the advantage of being able to draw on the expertise of a wide range of employees. However, these teams can be slow to make decisions because of the need to get input from all team members.

Quality improvement teams are formed to identify and solve problems with quality. These teams typically consist of employees from different departments who have knowledge about the problem area. Quality improvement teams have the advantage of being able to identify problems quickly. However, these teams may lack the authority to implement changes.

It's clear from these examples that no two teams are alike, and the flexibility of how teams can be structured is a powerful utility for productivity. However, there are fundamentals that exist within each team. Fundamental needs of team members, fundamental factors that contribute to their success, and fundamental drivers of motivation.

DOI: 10.4324/9781003177753-8

Research has spanned across all these types of teams, in varied industries and outlines the unique factors which contribute to the different teams' performance. For example, some team scientists have recently taken their research to space, informing NASA about how astronaut teams should be managed given the long-term exposure of members to each other in tight spaces and the lack of escape mechanisms during missions (Salas et al., 2015).[1]

No matter whether you are a team working on a Christmas marketing campaign or going to space – there is still the need for basic things such as clarity of roles, positive team cohesion, and working toward a collective goal. While these may remain the same, the team of the future will look very different to the teams we know today. I'm not here to predict what they will look but one thing I am sure of is – they will be developed by the demands of new generations. Social trends which point to a lack of appetite for hierarchy, a need for flexibility, and a fearless commitment to one's passion and values – are fairly antithetical to most of the way teams are formed and function in today's organization.

Autonomy, I believe will play a fundamental role in the team of the future. Both on a collective level and an individual level. Autonomy in how we work, what we work on, and why we would work on it in the first place – three contributors to what I believe a future (probablyself-organizing) team would look like.

The concept of a 'Super Team', made popular by Deloitte,[2] is one which I believe will fortunately and unfortunately become an increasingly popular model. In the future, this team will not be part of any specific organization, but rather a uniquely qualified set of motivated (independent) individuals, who leverage their superior skillsets and their demand, to provide services to their specialized industries. No, it's not a consultancy I'm describing, this isn't a business, rather they are a self-forming group of high-performing individuals that may have worked at the same organization or met on a project in the past and have pulled together their collective strengths to dictate their price and proposal with little to no room for negotiation.

Another major factor in the emergence of the team of the future is the fact that its members will no longer be employed by one organization. In fact, PwC predicts that the number of US workers in full-time 'permanent' employment will drop to 9% of the workforce, by 2030.[3] This means that what a team of the future will look like, is very different to what teams today look like. This of course will impact the way projects are run and how teams are assembled for them. Most importantly, leadership needs to prepare for this new type of team, generation at work, and the way they prefer to work. Gone are the days of assigning people to projects or tasks that they don't care for, there's a revolution happening, and it's not looking good for hierarchal organizations and their micro-mangers.

Notes

1 "TEAM SCIENCE – Research, Technology, and Methods." 28 Jul. 2019, https://science-teams.com/
2 Superteams | Human Capital Trends | Deloitte Africa.
3 PwC future of work report (see references).

9 The human-centric organization[1]

We know and will explore deeper the importance of a people-first approach to projects, and the impact team cohesion has on team performance. But how do these ideas transform entire organizations?

Organizations of the future will need to be fully human-centric in order to thrive in the future of work. What does that mean? First and foremost, it means understanding and catering to the needs of employees. Not just catering, but prioritizing. Taking not just the 'customer first' approach, but the 'employee first' approach. Making the success and happiness of your people – your organization's number one *business* goal. Most companies don't include many people-related metrics as part of their annual or quarterly targets. But this will become common practice soon, not just best practice. The best organizations will be those that can create a work environment and culture that meets not just the needs of employees, but also their wants. Not just professionally, but also personally. And this won't be limited to full-time employees of course (if that will even exist).

To be successful in this shift, organizations will need to go beyond simply implementing new technologies and tools that help them connect with their employees. They will need to go beyond well-being programs and unlimited vacation days. They will need to rethink their approach entirely to HR and talent management, and truly put people first instead of profits. Of course, this will naturally lead to higher profits, as the research shows, the happier the employee, the happier the bottom line.[2]

Human-centric organizations are those that are able to design a workplace and culture that creates such a demand within the talent market that even kids will say 'I want to join that organization when I grow up!'. They will design organizations purposefully tailored to humans, not build organizations simply made up of them. So often the priorities of leaders and those of employees are vastly mismatched. Especially as a new generation of workers enter the workplace, it will be critical to have a deep understanding of their wants and needs and have them be part of architecting the workplace of the future. If you don't already have one, a good first step would be to create a 'Gen-Z advisory board'.

DOI: 10.4324/9781003177753-9

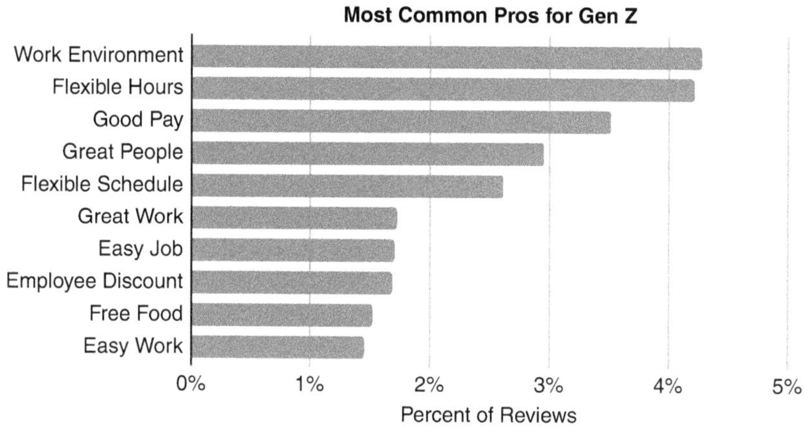

Figure 9.1 Most common pros for gen-z. (Glassdoor Economic Research).

One of my favorite quotes pertaining to change in the workplace specifically:

> 'In times of rapid change, experience could be your worst enemy.'
>
> J Paul Getty

Gen-Z and the future of work

By 2030, 30% of the workforce will be makeup of Gen-Z'ers,[3] and that number does not include millions of freelancers taking part in our projects. What's important to understand about Generation Z on a fundamental level is that they question everything. They are not afraid, to stand up, to challenge old-school ways of thinking or doing (no matter what level of authority you think you may have), and they won't give in until there is change. Of course, there are positives and negatives, but it is what it is and we're not going to change it. What we can do is listen, seek to understand, and build a future-proof organization around the ideals of the future workforce, as opposed to our existing ones.

Something that is different about this generation is, they bring their values and beliefs into the workplace. From the job hunt to the job exit, the causes they care about can't be brushed off with a raise.

Some of the top priorities amongst Gen-Z are:

- Purpose
- Sustainability
- Diversity and inclusion
- Equality[4]
- Mental Health

All positive strides forward for humanity no doubt, but organizations are feeling the impact of having to keep up with these values and initiatives in order to attract young talent. Gen-Z are already shaping organization's strategies, the products they build, how they build them, and who builds them.

Gen-Z do care about their careers and making money, but they won't sacrifice what they care about for it. Organizations will need to show that they don't either. The organizations of the future will need to have a purpose that goes beyond making money. By truly incorporating the values Gen-Z holds near and dear, and having a positive impact on the world, and their employees' lives – only then will they be able to attract and retain the best talent.

Starting with purpose

A good way to start is to go back to your company values.

If your value system contains meaningful beliefs and bigger picture pursuits, simply starting to instill them in your employees, and find ways they can contribute directly to these values – will build a stronger sense of shared purpose.

Purpose – Possibly the single most overlooked factor that contributes to an organization's success. Here's why: If an organization exhibits a high degree of purpose in its mission and objectives, prioritizing benefiting society, employees will more readily demonstrate purpose in their roles at work. They will become more engaged, while adding to their own personal sense of purpose in life as well.

A perfect example of this is when global giant Unilever decided to put purpose on par with the need for good profits through its ambitious Sustainable Living Plan, its employee engagement rose from the low 50s to the high 80s.[5] Though even more astonishing, the company also witnessed its market capitalization rise from €63 billion to over €100 billion while its earnings per share grew from 1.16 to almost 2.00.

My personal favorite is Salesforce. Their motto is *The Business of Business Is Improving the State of The World,* not 'to increase our bottom line' or, 'gain majority market share', and it's no surprise that consequently they have succeeded in accomplishing both. Their core values demonstrate the true driving factor behind their success.

Dan Ariely,[6] who has conducted numerous studies on the subject states: *'People want to feel like they're contributing', 'They want a sense of purpose, a sense that work itself has an impact'.*

Leverage their ideals, turning differences into drivers of change

- Disdain for authority can lead to flatter structures. A more diverse workforce and inclusive environment enhances cross-functional collaboration. In addition, ideas and voices that weren't given a platform now can contribute to innovation within the organization.

- Mental health awareness can lead to more effective wellness initiatives, including finding ways to reduce stress which will ultimately lead to increased organization productivity.
- Digital savviness can lead to doing away with legacy systems and processes, embracing digitization internally and externally, and creating a more agile organization.
- Need for flexibility can lead to a more productive organization as everyone's work schedule and location is optimized for them to get their best work done. (Added benefit is reduced office/utility overheads.)

I believe both business leaders and team leaders, that focus on enabling the new generation's ambitions in every way possible, will find success in their teams and organizations that may very likely exceed their expectations.

How it applies to teams

Granted not all these factors can be controlled or even influenced by team leaders, they may have no direct impact on the company's purpose. However, there is a lot that they do have an impact on. Whether it's being more inclusive in their team, promoting more sustainable practices in their projects, or prioritizing mental health in their team – there is enough to be done to contribute to building a human-centric, Gen-Z friendly organization. And it starts one team at a time.

We spoke about belonging in the first chapter and its importance in fostering an environment where people actually want to come to work and contribute to their team's success. Creating a team with a sense of belonging is easier said than done. It takes a lot of purposefulness and proactive behavior on the manager's part, and not always something that comes naturally to them.

This is where the power of behavior and decision sciences, combined with learning and development, can be an incredibly powerful vehicle to drive this change. We will speak more to this in the future section 'Nudges', in the meantime, here is a snippet on why it's important.

Notes

1 As I See it: The Autobiography of J. Paul Getty (Getty Publications – (Yale) 31 Mar. 2006.
2 "Research: How Employee Experience Impacts Your Bottom Line." 22 Mar. 2022, https://hbr.org/2022/03/research-how-employee-experience-impacts-your-bottom-line
3 The Gen Z Workforce: Who They Are, and What They Want.
4 What are Gen Z's Top Purpose-Driven Priorities? - Stylus 15 Insights into Gen Z, Purpose, and the Future of Work - WeSpire.
5 Unilever's Purpose And Sustainability Test Of Its Shareholders.
6 Dan Ariely - Wikipedia.

10 Infusing behavioral science into the workplace

When we talk about creating a more human-centric workplace, we would be remiss if we didn't further dissect and understand the human experience at work. Literally, what goes on in our brains before, during and after work. I don't see any other way to build a human-centric organization quite frankly. It would be like building a sanctuary for a species of Animals and designing the place without ever truly understanding that animal, how it behaves, what kind of environment it needs to survive, and how it interacts with other Animals.

There are many low-hanging fruits that team leads themselves can take into practice, and one of my favorites is incorporating humor into our daily work and team collaboration. We know that happiness at work correlates with increased productivity, but what about laughter? Surely that is a big symptom and even driver of happiness? Well, it is. There have been significant studies around this topic, proving that humor can reduce stress,[1] burnout and has an overall significant impact on an individual and team's functioning. There was even a correlation between individuals who displayed humor in their communication and their paycheck! As a comedy fanatic, I am biased to this one, but who doesn't like to laugh?

More so than just the understanding of the human, is the need to drive positive, bias-free decision-making amongst them – when it matters. This is truly where the power of behavioral science and team behavior insights within your organization can revolutionize the way that people work together. Ultimately work and just interacting with other humans is a series of thousands of micro-decisions and if we can improve them by just 10%, the outcomes will be much more significant than how small that percentage may seem.

Note

1 How Humor Can Reduces the Stress Caused by the Pandemic.

DOI: 10.4324/9781003177753-10

11 Where does this leave us?

So, what does this all mean for the future of work? Well, there's no doubt that organizations will need to start putting their people first. Not just employees, but everyone they work with. From customers, to suppliers, to partners. Everyone.

They need to start by not only looking inward at their own values and purpose, but also looking at who is at work (Gen-Z), what they want out of it, (purpose etc.), and how can we make it such an experience that our organization becomes one that is irresistible. An organization whose workforce doesn't simply live for their weekends and PTO but is excited to go to work on a Monday morning.

The reason we're including organizational discourse in a book about teams and projects is because there really is no difference. What I seek in an organization, I seekin my team and my manager. I don't leave only my organization, but I leave my team and my manager. Organizations need to really emphasize and dedicate resources to empowering team leaders and teams themselves to manage and drive this change. The future of work is teams, and the future of work is now.

DOI: 10.4324/9781003177753-11

12 Team performance

The fundamentals of high-performing teams

One of the most widely researched topics in organizational psychology and business management – what truly makes a great team, great? Hordes of research exist on the topics of team performance, be it academic research, private institutions, or the Fortune 500 themselves. Even in virtual team performance, the research dates to the 1960s – so the new global phenomenon of 'remote working', isn't really that new, after all some companies have been entirely remote for over two decades.

We know that no team is alike, as we've covered. Teams evolve and go through periods of change; dynamics shift and entire projects collapse solely on the foundation of team dysfunction. There are however certain fundamental qualities which are found across high-performing teams, and although to most of you reading these won't be new – I am implored to state some of them as this section covers high-performance teams:

- Clarity (roles, goals, and tasks)
- A common sense of purpose
- Emotional well-being (stress, work-life balance)
- Sense of belonging
- High levels of accountability
- Ownership of one's work
- Autonomy
- Continuous learning
- Alignment
- Agility/Adaptability
- Healthy conflict
- Empathetic leadership
- Psychological safety
- Mutual respect and trust

Of course, you won't find all these traits in every high-performance team, and the different contexts of team and project play a large part in the

DOI: 10.4324/9781003177753-12

weighting of each factor influencing the results of that team. However, it's vital for senior and functional leaders to know these traits on the back of their hands. To build a high-performance organization, one ought to know how to build and sustain a high-performing team. Thus, the repetitiveness of this topic and these traits is not without yield.

As we've touched on and will continue to (since it's conveniently the topic of this book), the social and emotional cohesion of the team is not to be underestimated when it comes to predicting performance. This is no longer what some people call 'the soft stuff', and if you hear a colleague respond with this phrase – RED FLAG.

Virtual team performance

When it comes to virtual teams, although much of the core principles remain the same, there are a whole new set of factors to consider when it comes to monitoring and enabling their performance. Without going into the complexities, I will say the one thing virtual team performance demands is proactive leadership and purposeful management. Despite its many benefits and wonders, it is undoubtedly more difficult to lead virtual teams. And when things start to slip, they are a lot harder to pick up than an in-person team. I've felt that pain first hand.

What's interesting is that the spectrum of virtual teams, the nuance of each team's virtuality level plays a crucial factor in determining what will make them successful or not. The range can go from a team dispersed globally, across multiple time zones that work primarily asynchronously. To teams that work remotely for a few days of the week. A team's degree of virtuality impacts their dynamics, communication requirements, and risks. For this reason, a tailored and personalized approach should be seriously considered when building and leading different types of virtual teams and projects.

Three pillars we found in recent research on virtual team effectiveness were:

1 **Social Cohesiveness**
This can be described as a shared liking of each other in the group, emotional bonds of friendship and closeness among group members. When managing a virtual team, significant emphasis should be put on building relationships and social cohesion, especially in the initial stage of the team development process.

2 **Team Trust**
It was also found that team trust is even more important for teams with a high level of virtuality, and it's been proven that virtual teams with high intra-team trust outperform teams where trust is low. Highly trusting teams also display higher levels of not only team performance, but also organizational commitment, information-sharing, and team learning.

This trust allows members to suspend judgment about others, thus helping prevent potential misunderstandings and conflicts that may occur due to the nature of virtual communication be more text driven and asynchronous.

3 **Information Sharing**
This refers to the extent to which a team utilizes its individual members' knowledge and expertise for the overall benefit of the team. This obviously means that the extent to which a team effectively shares information plays a considerable role in team performance. Sharing knowledge and information in a transparent and frequent manner is a vital component of virtual team success. In addition, it is important in the development of trust and social cohesion, which in turn increases team performance.

Creating a clear team charter or 'ways of working' as it's being called now is a good way to outline the basis for how the team should access and share information effectively throughout their time together.

Naturally, promoting a culture of transparency within your team goes without saying, and that starts at the top.

13 Servant leadership and team performance

The balance between building and maintaining work processes and building and maintaining work relationships is the mastery of the million-dollar manager. Having a strong emphasis on deadlines and boundaries versus being a visionary style leader are sometimes conflicting traits within managers; and that's exactly where leadership development and self-growth plays their part. Working on our weaknesses and leveraging our strengths as leaders, not once off, but continuously. No one ever said leading people toward a shared positive outcome (without pissing anyone off) was easy.

Although coined in 1970,[1] the concept of servant leadership has taken the business world by storm in recent years and it's no surprise, given that we just spoke about new generational needs and a shifting approach to the workplace. Employees who work under servant leaders enjoy their job more and are less likely to leave their companies.[2] But it's no easy feat and doesn't come naturally to most managers to act as 'servants' to their staff, in fact it doesn't come naturally to most humans to prioritize the needs of others so vividly before our own.

We've spoken about the importance of teams understanding each other and managers understanding their teams, but perhaps less spoken of is managers understanding managers. I believe this is the first step toward servant and empathetic leadership is self-awareness. To know one's weaknesses is the greatest strength of all. This isn't a book on leadership, there are enough out there, and I don't claim to have mastered it by any stretch, but one thing I can attest to is since doing the work to go inward, and really understand who I am, how I interact, and what are my shortcomings – I have most certainly become a better leader than when I started.

Notes

1 https://www.greenleaf.org/what-is-servant-leadership/
2 https://officeneedle.com/servant-leadership-statistics/

DOI: 10.4324/9781003177753-13

14 Sports psychology and team performance

Research in sports psychology can do far more than help us understand the makings of a winning team. This growing field also empowers countries and coaches to increase their efficacy by applying the tactics of other academic disciplines to their strategies, using insights drawn from sociology, neuropsychology, and behavioral science to create consistently high-performing teams.

Unsurprisingly, there's a lot of overlap between what we know about workplace teams and what we know about sports teams. But when it comes to conducting research and sharing lessons learned, there's not a lot of crossovers between the fields – pun intended.

As an avid sports fan, I'd like to highlight a few of the lessons we can transplant from the world of sports into the world of business, and why we ought to be encouraging more cross-pollination between the two. To the American readers – forgive me in advance if most of my examples are from Football (Soccer) or Cricket.

Continuous measurement means continuous improvement

It's no wonder that sports analytics has become a multibillion-dollar industry – when teams use data-driven strategies to make decisions, they unsurprisingly experience higher win rates.[1] I'll be focusing more on the on-field, player-related data, than opposition data or game simulation, etc. In a data-driven team, everything about an individual player's performance is tracked, both in training sessions, on game day, and in between. Crucially, the purpose of this detailed analysis isn't to penalize players with their own performance data – it's to help them better understand themselves and each other, and to identify areas for improvement. There's a symbiotic relationship between players and their club, and that sense of mutual understanding is why you don't see the same kind of suspicion about employee analytics in workplaces.

Whether or not an organization can successfully pull something like this off is completely dependent on their culture and their priorities. While both

DOI: 10.4324/9781003177753-14

involve data-gathering technology and data analytics, giving an employee a Fitbit so they can monitor their health is not the same thing as installing spyware on their laptop to track their screen time and count keystrokes.

Just like charity, performance starts at home!

In sports, tracking player health doesn't stop when they leave the locker room and head home – sleep and nutrition are one of the most important determinants of[2] player health, and neither of those happen on the sports field. While the office is a different arena, performance in the workplace is just as driven by your life outside work.

Therefore, I would encourage managers to engage with their teams about their health in a more proactive way, with an emphasis on self-care strategies that will improve not only their performance, but also their sense of well-being overall.

Forward-thinking companies have tried various strategies to improve employee health, whether it be through behavioral science strategies like nudging and reward programs, or company perks such as gym memberships.

Team performance from the sports field to the workplace

If we want to draw on sports psychology to improve our workplaces, we need to look at the characteristics[3] of a winning team:

- Team Cohesion
    - Yes, here it is again. And for good reason, there's a direct correlation between how cohesive teams are and how well they perform. Even as a spectator you can sense which teams have this, in the way they play, celebrate, and interact off the field. Every other factor that makes a team great relies on cohesion. It's everything, and smart coaches focus on it from day one.
- Clarity
    - To expand on the first factor, winning teams have complete clarity on their mission both from manager and club, beyond just 'let's go win tournaments' – Italy's road to winning the Euros is[4] a great example of this. Everyone is clear on the direction of the manager and there is alignment on what's expected of everyone in order to achieve their goals. This collective focus breeds a powerful force of winners.
- Trust
    - It's painfully evident when players on the field don't trust one another – you can see it in their style of play – and there's a reason that the trust fall is *the* quintessential team-building activity. In some sports, the reliance on your team members to catch you when you fall isn't even metaphorical. Whether it be a line out in

Rugby or a cheerleading routine – teammates need to trust that they won't let them break a limb (or their neck) on the way down from a jump.

- Psychological Safety
    - On the sports field, losing and making mistakes are unavoidable realities, even for those at the very top of the game. As a rule, professional athletes are naturally competitive – a keen desire to win is just part of the athlete's psyche – which makes losing all the more painful for them. How this sense of failure is handled by the team – as individual players and as a collective – is an extremely important factor in the makings of a good team. Accepting and overcoming failure is a team sport, and players will only be able to process these feelings together if they are in an environment of psychological safety. A great example of this, was when Bukayo Saka,[5] the youngest Englishman to start a semi-final of a major tournament, missed the winning penalty in the Final of the Euros[6] and instead of being berated by his teammates and manager, he was hugged, held, and comforted when all he could do was cry, holding his head in shame. Off the sports field, the importance of fostering psychological safety in the workplace is well-established, as research has consistently demonstrated the impact it has on organizational performance and innovation.
- Radical Candor
    - As a spectator, you might have heard players or managers screaming at one another during the game, or right after. It can seem hostile, even vicious – but that the shouting isn't being taken personally. Because it's not meant to be: the beauty of feedback in sports is that criticism can be brutal without being personal, and that it's delivered with the ultimate goal of improvement in mind. On the sports field, mistakes are noticed immediately, so the feedback loops are instant, and improvements have to happen in real time. This isn't the case in business, where it can take months before a performance issue is uncovered. By that time, it's usually too late to fix it.
- Team Retrospection
    - No matter whether it was a win or a loss, top teams will re-watch their games as individuals and as a team, in order to self-assess and identify areas for improvement. This team trait is found in elite military teams as well, after a mission they review every move and conduct a lessons learned exercise. The agile movement has pioneered 'retrospectives' into the world of business (although primarily in software development), however there is still a growing need for a better process whereby teams can easily and productively self-assess on a high frequency.

- Growth Mindset[7]
  - How do tier 3 teams beat league champions? Well, I don't think any analyst can be confident in a logical explanation for some of sport's greatest upsets, but one thing is for sure – they believed they could. There are some amazing and wholesome underdog tales in sports, whether an individual Olympian or a national team – these tales prove that 'impossible' is just a word in the dictionary. (The rise of Leicester City Football Club, from small club to Premier League Champions is an inspiring example of the power of growth mindset.[8])
- Rest and Work-life Balance
  - For athletes, recovering is just as important as training. It's mandatory – at times, coaches must force players to rest, as part of a long-term strategy to conserve energy and avoid burnout. Prevention is always the better option, which is why post-match recovery is given priority in the sporting world. In the workplace, rest mandates tend to happen post-burnout. As we all know, by then it's too late and attrition rates are likely climbing. What about rest mandates before burnout? Hmm.

A good manager is a great coach

Isn't it interesting that in sports the manager is called 'coach' by the players and in business we keep seeing the words 'managers need to become coaches' – surely there are some lessons here to be learned?

Something all winning teams have in common is the unique relationship between coach and team. I touched on the feedback element earlier, which is obviously the hallmark of a great coach, but I'd like to focus on what some might call 'the soft stuff' – which is hardly *soft*, given the enormous impact it has.

Leadership Empathy: While there are many elements that make up a great coach, perhaps none are more crucial than having the ability to connect with, understand, and empower their players. Jurgen Klopp is[9] a master at this and this trait has surely accounted for a lot of his success in Football.

Mutual Respect: Regardless of whatever minor disagreements or public feuds might mark their history, winning teams have a profound and unmistakable sense of respect for their managers. This is especially apparent in teams that have had years-long winning streaks. Sir Alex Ferguson is[10] a prime example, a man respected by both friend and foe. The same respect must be reciprocated. When players see or feel that their coach loses respect for them, they end up leaving the club.

With these two traits covered, the coach-player relationship can blossom into a safe space and allow for the most important job a coach is contracted to do – confidence building. Beyond the need to inspire and motivate the team as a whole, building individual players' confidence is paramount for coaches to get right in order to build winning teams. Countless wonder stories are told by players and coaches alike, of how they were in the trenches emotionally and mentally, and their coach pulled them out and slowly built up their self-belief off the field, which in turn improved their performance on the field.

It's no surprise to me that many former coaches have gone on to become wildly successful business. Bill Campbell[11] is the perfect example of a successful transition from the sports field into the business world. Before he became one of the greatest leadership coaches of our time, Campbell was the coach of a Varsity football team. I've gained much from reading Campbell's story and taking his lessons in management to heart. Business management, to Campbell, is people management; leadership isn't about what you can make people do, but how you make people feel. Leaders who figure this out early on are the ones to find genuine and holistic success.

As seen, there are clearly many lessons and attributes we can derive from sports when it comes to team performance in the workplace, and despite some of them being repetitive, I think it's fascinating that whether you're 11 people kicking a ball toward the same goal posts, or 11 people working on building an app – the fundamental drivers of performance are not very different.

Notes

1 For these students, using data in sports is about more than winning games (theconversation.com).
2 the most important determinants.
3 It's worth noting that a team can possess many of these qualities and still not be a top-performing team, in addition to a fantastic team spirit and winning mentality, teams do need sufficient resources in order to acquire and retain top talent, management, facilities, and of course fan base.
4 Italy's road to winning the Euros.
5 "Bukayo Saka - Wikipedia." https://en.wikipedia.org/wiki/Bukayo_Saka. Saka Image Credit: EuroSport.
6 missed the winning penalty in the Final of the Euros.
7 "Growth Mindset | Psychology Today." https://www.psychologytoday.com/us/basics/growth-mindset
8 The rise of Leicester City Football Club, from small club to Premier League Champions.
9 Jurgen Klopp.
10 Sir Alex Ferguson.
11 Bill Campbell.

15 The secret superpower of team intelligence

An experiment was conducted in 1906 by a man named Francis Galton,[1] with results that give us a fascinating glimpse into the nature of collective intelligence. Attending a country fair in Plymouth, Galton watched as 787 villagers were asked to guess the weight of an ox for a cash prize. No one got it exactly right, but when he calculated the average of all 787 responses, he found something very strange: It was only one pound off the correct answer.

It turns out this wasn't an isolated incident. The phenomenon Galton observed has been dubbed 'the wisdom of crowds', and in the century since, we've seen many cases of crowds being smarter than their individual members. In fact, it's been proven that a crowd of laypeople will usually be more reliable than an individual expert: Large groups of people have best experts in everything from forecasting the outcome of the English Premier League[2] to winning game shows.[3] This odd ability is the foundation of *prediction markets* – markets based around traders betting on the likelihood of future events[4] – which have proven effective in predicting everything from the spread of infectious diseases[5] to fluctuations in the demand for second-hand car parts.[6]

Crowds and teams are remarkably similar. That's good news for managers and organizations.

It might not seem like that's the case at first glance: Where a crowd is a spontaneous and ungovernable organism, a team is traditionally a carefully constructed group assembled for a specific purpose. But here, the wisdom of the crowd is really just a spontaneous, organic manifestation of the collective intelligence great team leaders know how to leverage. In other words, team intelligence and crowd wisdom are built on the same foundations, and once you understand the building blocks of a good crowd, you can apply those principles to running better teams.

So, while a team and a crowd aren't quite the same thing, there's one crucial factor they have in common: Their collective intelligence can be far greater than that of their individual members and their leaders.

Are crowds always, right? Absolutely not. In fact, it's worth recognizing why and how collective intelligence could fail. Understanding how the

DOI: 10.4324/9781003177753-15

wrong conditions can hamstring the potential of a crowd tells us what we need to do if we're trying to create the conditions for team intelligence to work.

Why do some crowds fail? There's a long answer to that question, but experts say the wisdom of a crowd comes down to a few important and interrelated factors: diversity, independence, and trust.

- **Diverse crowds are smarter:** Diversity here means diversity of opinion. If the members of your crowd already agree on everything, they're more likely to become a biased hive mind and their collective opinion won't diverge much from the status quo.
- **Diverse opinions require independent thinking:** If you're press-ganged into 'puppeting' the people around you, your thoughts stop being your own. Independent thinking inevitably involves some degree of conflict – and that's a good thing. Smart collectives are not unwaveringly harmonious. In fact, their best decisions come from conflict and contestation. Conflict between independent thinkers should be healthy and intellectually stimulating, not toxic and creatively stifling. For productive conflict, a strong social and psychological infrastructure is essential.
- **Independent thinking requires trust:** People can only express divergent opinions if they trust that the group will treat them with fairness. People need to know that it's not just *acceptable* to disagree with other members of the group, but *desirable*. This requires a sense of *psychological safety* – the belief that you won't be punished or humiliated for asking questions, speaking up about your ideas, raising your concerns, or admitting your mistakes.

Could this be why some teams fail?

Teams often fail for the same reasons crowds fail: They lack the psychological and social infrastructure to unlock collective intelligence.

- **They aren't as diverse as they'd like to think:** If you have a team rich in diverse opinions but only ever hear the voices of the strongest personalities – the most confident and loudest members of the group – you will never reap the full benefits of team intelligence. Keeping tabs on who's talking the most and how everyone is feeling and how their different personalities feed into the team dynamic requires superhuman emotional intelligence, a lot of time, and a fair amount of mind-reading. It's unrealistic and unfair to expect this from managers. Despite our best intentions, we're all subject to unconscious biases, and none of us (to the best of our knowledge) are telepaths. It's important to note that social-historical forces and unconscious prejudices are present in all workplaces, and among even the most well-intentioned people. If you want to work in a team that is actually diverse, you have to think about more than just who you're hiring – you need to consider whether there's a foundation of mutual trust, respect, and inclusivity within your team.

- **They don't like it when you disagree:** Like smart crowds, diverse teams of independent thinkers draw strength from disagreement, which requires a sense of mutual trust. That trust is what we call psychological safety, and it's something that's sorely lacking in many teams. Unfortunately, it can be incredibly difficult to create the ideal conditions for psychological safety, and this puts immense pressure on managers who rely solely on intuition and their gut instincts about what their teams need. As James Surowiecki[7] points out in his book on the matter, the wisdom of a crowd also depends on whether there's a mechanism in place for turning the private judgments of individuals into collective decisions. This is part of what we did with Perflo by creating a dedicated system that collects and analyzes anonymous team suggestions and input automatically throughout a team's lifecycle, we enabled leaders to make decisions based on data rather than guesswork (Figure 15.1).

People need to be the priority

I've said it before, and I'll say it again. The most exciting idea we can gather from the wisdom of crowds is that successful collective decision-making starts with understanding people and creating the conditions they need to thrive.

Applying that people-first principle to team leadership and harnessing the wisdom of the crowd in the workplace requires managers to rely more on

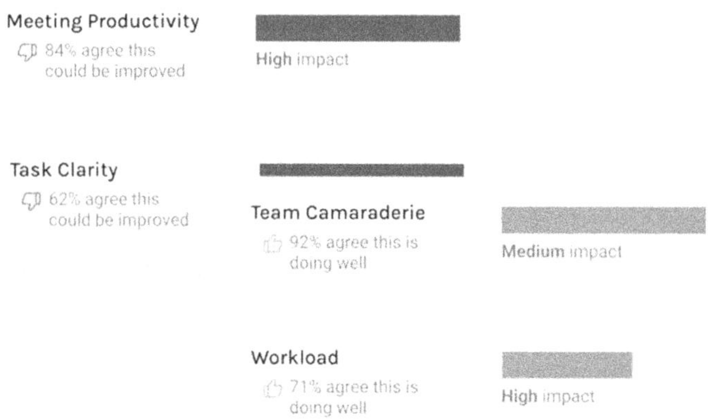

Figure 15.1 Perflo – Team feedback.

the invaluable collective intelligence their teams have to offer. A team is always more than the sum of its parts.

Assessing performance > developing teams

Assessing performance in knowledge workers has been a complex and much debated topic over the last few decades, with ever-changing research, opinions, and methodologies. There are so many complexities beyond the binary performance metrics which are usually measurable in units and numbers.

When trying to measure team performance, you only find more complexities, variables, and uncertainty due to the nature of how teams work together and their interdependentness. Furthermore, looking at the influencing *dynamics* or *events* on team performance is very different from looking at the influencing *individuals* on team performance. Nevertheless, it is a non-negotiable aspect of management to find appropriate measures of performance to track whether goals are being achieved or not. Unfortunately, a lot of this happens when it's already too late and the team is noticeably disrupted.

So just like sports teams, and just like individual humans, workplace teams need regular checkups to ensure that they are healthy and performing effectively. Regular checkups will catch deviations and enable a corrective course of action. When teams begin to lose their ability to function at a high level of effectiveness, shown by declining performance, many of them never quite pull out of this downward cycle and continue to exist as a collection of individuals masquerading as a team.

Many managers fail to differentiate between what teams are supposed to do and what the team is really doing. What I'm talking about is a form of team-based preventative medicine by consistently checking the vital signs. It's the well-known argument, or rather fact 'prevention is the best form of medicine'.

Traditionally, there are standard forms of health checks in teams which primarily consist of pulse surveys, which most of the time are not continuous or intelligent but rather contain a dull set of repetitive questions which don't yield any incredibly insightful insights. One could argue that agile retrospectives are the answer to preventative medicine within teams, however, let's face it – 99% of the time these meetings are talking about the work and not the team. And similarly, to what we spoke about previously on team intelligence – it's usually the same set of folks who are contributing their thoughts.

We are yet to find the holy grail of team development.

To truly get a more accurate picture of team performance we need to find and leverage new and improved ways of measuring and developing teams. Not to score them and penalize them, but to help them grow and develop. Traditionally, leaders and consultants have turned to one-off assessments to evaluate team performance and effectiveness.

Team assessments

When it comes to team development, an assessment is the first step in understanding the current state of the team. It can help identify areas of strength and weakness. Team assessments come in different forms, but all aim to provide insights into how well the team is working together.

There are many reasons why organizations might use a team assessment. Common reasons include:

- To diagnose team problems and determine the root cause
- To measure team effectiveness and identify areas for improvement
- To assess team dynamics and identify potential conflict areas
- To evaluate team roles and responsibilities
- To benchmark team performance against others

A team assessment should go beyond simply measuring satisfaction or engagement. It ought to provide a more in-depth look at the team dynamics and how the team functions together. This information can then be used to help the team leader develop a plan for improvement.

The problem with current team assessment methods

There are however several problems with team assessments used nowadays which I will elaborate on and bring some recent research-backed alternatives. The solution we propose will help measure and increase team effectiveness in a much more seamless way, resulting in an actual immediate impact on team performance and engagement, and not just a score to complain about.

1. A survey or health check is not a science-backed method of assessment.
2. The majority of 'team assessments' are actually individual assessments (personality, skills, etc.).
3. They are reactive – oftentimes only being executed after there are performance or dynamic issues in the team.
4. They are point-in-time – measuring what is happening in that present moment but not reflecting an accurate picture (things change daily, hourly).
5. Not all teams function equally – so it isn't always a one size fits all approach.
6. Statistical accuracy – asking questions on an individual level in group evaluations does not always accurately reflect the team's consensus and sentiment.
7. Who executes them – a lot of times you focus on only the things you know are current issues or blockers in the team and leave out what may be important as well (looking to confirm your beliefs as opposed to being open to unknown results).

8 They are tedious, boring, and no one likes doing them.
9 They cost money – sometimes requiring external consultants.
10 Taking action – having the results but not knowing what to do after.

Another important thing to keep in mind is that some team members may be much more engaged and active, while others might be very disengaged or 'checked-out'. It's quite possible for one team member to score incredibly high on an assessment, while other members score nothing above average. This can cause team leaders to think they have a great team on their hands when in fact there is a major problem with individual motivation levels within the group.

Getting deeper into the psychology of it all – many of these 'tests' require participants to use their unconscious mind instead of conscious thought processes, which isn't how teams actually perform tasks. Teams are dynamic environments where people must work together to solve problems – if they are not conscious of how they are functioning, then these team assessments can't be effective in measuring or increasing their true performance.

Finally, many teams tend to perform better when the group is left with some degree of ambiguity – this is often referred to as 'constructive ambiguity'. It's hard for assessment tests to incorporate this phrase because it doesn't directly test any one behavior or skill set. This means that most team assessments are done in a very black-and-white manner.

In order for team assessments to be effective, it's important that they:

- Be tailored specifically toward the team (and project currently working on).
- Incorporate both conscious and unconscious thought process.
- Allow room for constructive ambiguity.
- Are not a 'one-off' event, rather ongoing.
- Adapt and grow with the team intelligently (this is where AI can be powerful).
- Provide value to individual team members.
- Provide immediate and actionable solutions.
- Focus more on team dynamics, as opposed to individual personalities.

An alternative approach

Continuous, dynamic, and (fully) team-based micro-assessments.

Continuous micro-assessments that focus exclusively on the team as a collective is an extremely powerful and untapped vehicle for team measurement and improvement. Being dynamic, they evolve with the development of the team and the project they may be working on – this provides contextual insights to leaders in the flow of work and does not bore team members with repetitive or irrelevant questions (Figure 15.2).

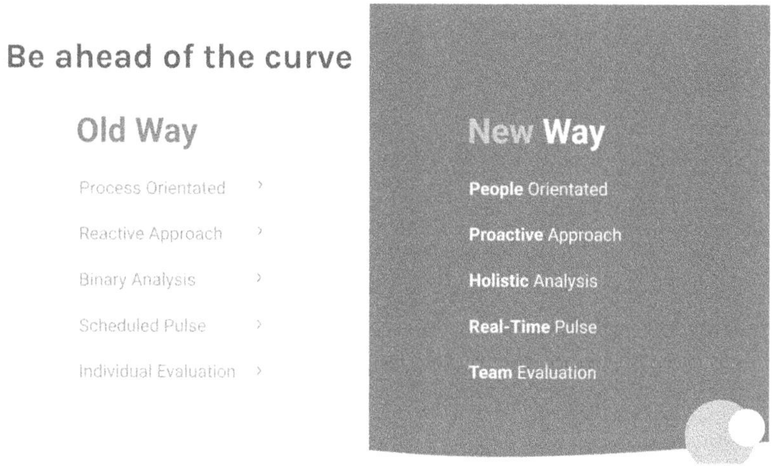

Figure 15.2 Perflo – the new way.

The best way is to include the team in forming part of the micro-assessments; what are our team values, what behaviors do we want to drive that will make us successful. By collectively answering these questions, you will arrive at a much more meaningful set of measurements, and you will be able to detect and prevent issues and risks that may have already been privy to your team. Additionally, the exercise is a form of team evaluation as you start to uncover topics that may have been repressed until now.

Team development takes more than just team assessments – it's a continuous journey that should be revisited on a regular basis. However, team assessments can be an extremely valuable tool in the team leader's arsenal, if used correctly. By incorporating team values, communication styles, and risk factors into the assessment process, team leaders can get a much more accurate representation of their team's true performance and dynamics.

We will dive deeper into the 'how' of these micro-assessments in the next chapter 'Team Analytics'.

Continue with personality-based assessments

I do want to emphasize that we are not saying there is no value in the individual-based assessments, there certainly is. It is incredibly useful to understand each other when working together in a team and identify early on, the potential sources of conflict that may occur, and learn how one another communicates. We believe these are just another tool in a team's toolbox for optimal performance, and they can be administered even after the team has been formed, it's never too late to understand one another better.

Who is responsible for team development?

The team leader is ultimately responsible for team development, but it's important that the team be involved in the process as well. This will help foster a sense of ownership and responsibility among team members and help them feel like they are an integral part of the team.

The role of L&D in team development is to provide the team leader with the necessary resources and tools to foster team development. This includes providing training on team dynamics, providing assessments and tools that help measure team performance, and helping team leaders set achievable goals for the team. L&D can also help by facilitating dialogues between team members to help them understand their team dynamics and how they can improve team performance.

What will the future hold?

The future of team development is a question that is still up for debate. However, there are some key trends that are emerging that could have a big impact on how teams work together in the future.

One such trend is, leveraging the capabilities brought about by artificial intelligence, to enhance the automation and efficiency of team development. Not to remove the human element, but to allow us to react faster to team critical issues and alert the right human to take action, without relying on a manual process. Predictive analytics combined with intelligent nudges will play a large part in this space and become the norm I imagine.

The move away from the individual and toward the team in the workplace will continue to drive new innovations in both processes and tools when it comes to measuring and increasing *team* performance.

As business becomes more competitive, more virtual, and more uncertain – the need for teams to work together effectively becomes more and more important. In order to stay ahead of the competition, businesses need to start to focus on team enablement, which quite simply is the process of ensuring that teams have all the tools and resources they need to be successful. Measurement and development – being core fundamentals to their success.

Organizations that focus on enabling teams will be more successful than those that don't. Simple. Teams make up the organism of the organization and collectively, their development, is the development of the organization.

Notes

1 "The Wisdom of Crowds by Francis Galton - Psychology." https://www.all-about-psychology.com/the-wisdom-of-crowds.html
2 forecasting the outcome of the English Premier League.
3 winning game shows.
4 traders betting on the likelihood of future events.
5 spread of infectious diseases.
6 fluctuations in the demand for second-hand car parts.
7 "James Surowiecki - Wikipedia." https://en.wikipedia.org/wiki/James_Surowiecki

16 From assumption to data – introducing team analytics

On a day-to-day level – Team Analytics empowers team leaders to *act* rather than *react*; to know what support or resources their team needs, as soon as they need it. We don't want to wait until the exit interview to find out why a team member was unhappy in our organization or wait till the end of a project to find out why it failed to meet expectations – when it's already far too late to fix what's broken. So, we should be doing everything in our power to create the conditions for proactive leadership and build environments and teams that people want to be part of. This starts with understanding our people in a way that is deliberate and systematic, based on their real needs rather than our own often-times, faulty assumptions.

As we discussed in the beginning of this book, data is used to make decisions in every other part of the organization, yet when it comes to building, managing, and leading teams, very little team-related data is used to make decisions, large or small. This mismatch remains a mystery to me. But here I am, together with Peter, writing about it, in the hopes that people can implement these concepts into their organization and see powerful transformation (Figure 16.1).

It starts with getting curious

If managers want to create better workplaces, they need to stop assuming that they already know what matters to their team members and what's going wrong in their teams. In a study by McKinsey,[1] leaders were asked why employees were leaving in droves – and the top three reasons they identified were compensation, work-life balance, and physical or emotional health. But when employees were asked the same question, most responded that they were considering resignation because they didn't feel valued by their organizations or their managers, and because they didn't feel a sense of belonging at work. Leadership was getting it all wrong.

It is becoming increasingly clear that leaders don't know what their people want – employees don't *only* care about better compensation or more reasonable workloads. A recent survey of American knowledge workers found that 50% of respondents wanted to leave their current job,

DOI: 10.4324/9781003177753-16

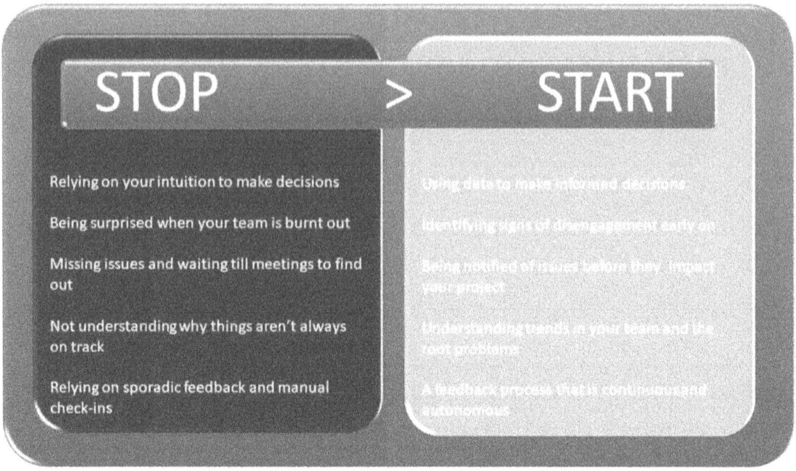

Figure 16.1 Transformation stop starts.

with the desire for location flexibility[2] post-pandemic being the most significant reason. Another survey[3] showed that nine out of ten employees would take a pay cut if it meant doing a more meaningful job – affirming what we mentioned before on Gen-Z's priorities. Employees want more than salary increases and days off: they also want more inclusivity, flexibility, and caring workplace environments. Organizations that make faulty assumptions about these issues will inevitably make ineffective changes. The crucial question, then, is how we can stop making these false assumptions.

We need more than good intentions and vague curiosity if we want to change our workplace culture. We need a systematic approach to understanding employees, and on a continuous and contextual basis. This is what I've spent a few years developing at Perflo; empowering team members to continuously communicate their needs and concerns directly to their managers, in a way that is safe, honest, and actionable. And of course, empowering managers to understand their teams better, faster, and more honestly.

Because this approach focuses on teams rather than entire organizations, the feedback loop is sped up, managers are able to make the right decisions faster – and most importantly – they make those decisions based on *data*, not assumptions. We drew heavily on the research on the psychology of teams. In addition, we leveraged behavioral science techniques to increase impact by driving the desire to take action swiftly.

The reason I'm so passionate about a data-driven solution is the fact that it results in team insights that are immediately actionable and containing a lot less bias. In this way, good intentions can be translated into effective changes that make employees feel properly valued, really cared for, and meaningfully engaged.

Turning curiosity into understanding

Positive team outcomes and a healthy organizational culture rely on inclusivity, respect, and honesty; team members need to feel that their voices are both *heard* and *valued*. That's not always easy, but it is always important – if we don't start listening, we'll keep operating on faulty assumptions, making the wrong decisions, and losing our people at unsustainable and unacceptable rates.

- Hearing voices: To communicate honestly and make their voices heard, team members need to feel a sense of *psychological safety* – they need to know that they can speak up without fear of being punished or humiliated. Making a team an inclusive one and fostering a safe environment should be a top priority for managers. Promoting difference and disagreement doesn't only make for better work outcomes – it also means that team members feel a greater sense of ownership and involvement in their projects and have better relationships with their colleagues and managers. As studies have shown, feeling cared for is a crucial part of positive workplace culture[4] – and the first step in caring about someone is listening to them.

But simply listening isn't enough. Leveraging team feedback means basing your decisions on their insights. In other words: their voices don't just need to be *audible* to you – they need to really *matter*.

- Valuing voices: For team members' voices to matter, their insights have to ultimately guide their team leads' decision-making processes. Valuing someone's input isn't just about thinking it's important in an abstract sense. You have to translate your attitude into action.

But managers are only human.

It's easy enough to say that managers ought to hear and value their team's voices. The problem is that team leaders don't have superhuman empathy and unlimited time. Like everyone else, team leaders make assumptions and have blind spots and – as far as we can tell – none of them are mind readers. This is where the power technology, namely, team analytics comes into play.

Turning understanding into action

My belief is that curiosity, understanding, and action should be built into the work process at the ground floor – and that a systematic (yes, I know I've used it eight times already), continuous collection and analysis of team feedback, actions, and behaviors is the way to do it. Again, not eliminating the human touch, rather building the vehicle for the human touch to be faster and more overall impactful.

One of the reasons a data-driven approach is necessary is because it not only allows for voices to be heard anonymously, but it also eliminates the risk of team leads' misconceptions, biases, and blind spots which can create self-imposed narratives about what their teams think, value, and want. This is especially important in light of the massive increase in virtual and hybrid teams, as it's far more difficult to intuit someone's state of mind when you're only seeing them on a screen.

Through the continuous collection of anonymized micro-feedback, we make it possible for managers to listen to team members who might otherwise go unheard. The anonymity aspect is crucial as it encourages a sense of safety and honesty, and the opportunity to provide ongoing feedback means that managers aren't relying on the loudest voices and their own gut feelings to determine what's going on with their teams. I know managers are busy, so proactively sending behaviorally based nudges in Slack or Microsoft Teams to aid them in the process of team enablement is key to turning 'understanding into action' (more on nudges later). By listening – not assuming – managers create workplaces that don't push people out, but rather draw them together, developing that sense of belonging needed to achieve workplace satisfaction.

To sum up – For managers, team analytics is about using data to make decisions and not their intuition. Not discounting intuition, emotion, or empathy, but rather making empathy more easily accessible – and intuition more accurate.

Curiosity, understanding, and action on an organizational level

What happens when every team has its own continuous feed of insights pertaining to its effectiveness and performance? You get an organization that is infused with rich data, and in real-time. This is an incredibly powerful concept and one that excites me due to the tip of the iceberg of which we are on. I'm not talking about reporting data from project management tools, I'm talking about team analytics! It's a new layer of insights for 99% of organizations on the planet. And it's one that they desperately need to retain and engage top talent, and of course execute successful projects.

Team analytics can eliminate much of the stress leaders face when things are beginning to go wrong. Mostly because data doesn't lie. With team analytics, no one can cover up issues that are boiling up, or fabricate more optimistic team projections. Not the manager, the team member or the VP. This will allow early-stage detection and rectification across all areas of the organization. Looking ahead, after a process and tool for team analytics is in place – organizations can begin to build smarter teams according to previous data, plan better for major projects, and assign the right people to the job based on data, not availability. A powerful concept indeed.

Team analytics – what it is

Team analytics is the idea of taking a data-driven approach to managing and enabling teams – helping make data-driven decisions to optimally empower your team.

This data primarily comes from the team itself, via a qualitative feedback mechanism.

There are additional data sources that can be used to deeper analyze team effectiveness such as project management reporting, communication network data, and productivity data from various collaboration tools. The concept is to leverage both the quantitative and qualitative data that makes up the activity, behaviors and sentiment of a team in order to (as accurately as possible) measure, predict, and increase both performance and well-being in real-time. A healthy team is a high-performing team, so for me the well-being data is the performance data, there is no separation.

Team analytics – what it is not

The biggest misconception of 'Team Analytics' is that it is some sort of 'spy data'.

This couldn't be further from the truth and its intent. Sadly, there are some products that do monitor employee's digital activity to a ridiculously, and borderline illegal level – completely defeating the purpose of building trust and harmony within a team. Two things that define its effectiveness ironically. The team analytics we talk of here does not 'spy' on any employee, nor does it measure things like the time spent on which software, eye movements, number of strokes on a keyboard. All metrics we believe to be completely counter-productive, and neither do they accurately measure productivity.

I know I'm repeating myself, but it's important due to the skepticism (particularly of team members) – team analytics should seek to produce insights which help make teams and organizations more effective and not seek to evaluate and penalize individual employees' performance. A good way to tell if your team analytics practice is gearing toward the dark side of things is to ask yourself 'would I/we be comfortable sharing these insights with everyone in the team no matter what' – the idea is that no insight should require discreetness, and what the manager sees, the team sees. This isn't an HR tool, it's not a performance management tool – it's a team improvement and team health tool.

Team data, not individual data

I mean, it's in the name but there can be confusion since most team assessments are actually individual-based like we discussed. However, team analytics in this context should only contain team-level data and not individual-level data. Even when predicting attrition within a team, revealing individual data completely shatters the process of building a continuous feedback system with a team. Anonymity is critical to gleaning valuable insights. Yes, some (mature) teams will reveal personal suggestions made and feel safe to elaborate on the motives behind their feedback, however most teams aren't there yet. Communicating the anonymity element to employees is not a once-off event, nor is it an easy feat, albeit one that is a must in order to reap the true benefits of team analytics.

The implementation process is critical to get right, it sets the precedent for how teams should engage with this new (or improved) feedback mechanism. It is the single biggest factor in determining the success of such a program, even ahead of manager onboarding/training.

Getting insights to the right people when it matters

Companies have been collecting feedback and/or other important data in an attempt to understand and drive performance for years – But merely possessing it isn't enough if the data isn't delivered to the right people at the right time, it can't do more than help us understand problems after they've arisen.

I often give the example of your car dealership holding the data of your fuel gauge, and you didn't have real-time access to the data, but don't worry, when you run out of fuel, they'll be sure to let you know. The same is happening in organizations, primarily when it comes to people-related insights.

We believe people-related insights should be far more readily accessible to managers and their teams, and that they should be delivered much faster. After all, these are the people who work on the front lines every day; those who can make an immediate difference to an organization's performance. Starting with team performance and team well-being to ultimately achieve team success. In light of this, I decided to repurpose components of HR-related tools to create Perflo. To empower managers and their teams to set up and access their own team-generated insights allowing them to make strategic decisions to tackle issues as they arise, and not after they blow up. If a manager's team is out of sync, they need to know now – not next week or the end of the quarter. Without timely insights, managers are essentially left flying blind, unable to understand the human factors that impact team dynamics, performance, and engagement. The micro-assessments being built and designed exclusively for teams and the insights contextual to that team type, project, and stage of development.

Again, the intention is not for performance evaluation of individual team members but rather for it to be an efficient process to discover potential problems, collectively problem-solve, and increase team performance and its probability of success.

Empowering managers has never been more important

The world is changing at an increasingly fast pace. Since the Coronavirus pandemic has accelerated the transition to remote work and in-person

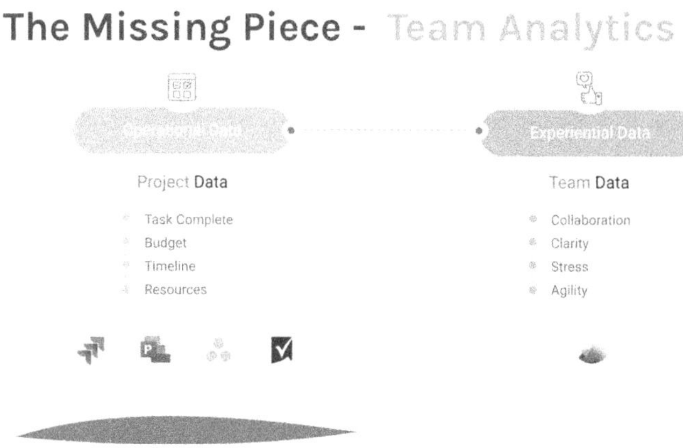

Figure 16.2 The missing piece – team analytics.

interactions (both formal and informal) have dramatically reduced, it has never been more important for managers to find ways to keep their fingers on the pulse regarding their team's performance and engagement. Working virtually will inevitably make issues harder to notice and will increase the likelihood of problems sneaking up on unsuspecting managers.

As the rate of change accelerates, organizations must become more agile. Those who can adapt rapidly will survive; those who aren't, won't. To make the right decisions swiftly, managers need data delivered in real-time. They need leading data points on team performance that can help them tackle issues as they arise – not lagging data points that highlight issues after they've come to the fore.

This all points toward the need for a new approach, and equipping managers with team analytics seems to me the most obvious one (Figure 16.2).

Why this is critical for managers of project-based teams

The need for real-time performance data is particularly pressing for managers of project-based teams. The way these cross-functional teams operate and the way they are assembled and disassembled means that they face greater uncertainty and urgency than functional teams do. As a result, a greater deal of agility is required from project-based teams.

Traditionally, managers of project teams have had access to a large body of process-related data, but not much people-related data, if any. When project teams become misaligned – which they do, regularly – managers usually don't know until it's too late. This is the primary reason many projects fail to deliver on time and within budget.

To succeed consistently in our projects, giving managers and teams the insights, they need to solve problems collectively, before they escalate, and to make more informed decisions, will be essential.

I truly believe and have seen that when managers are armed with team insights, they will not only be able to lead teams more effectively, but also make those crucial strategic decisions that have such a massive impact on an entire organization.[5]

Measure your weakness as a manager

It may surprise you, but I am not a natural empath, and that translates when I manage teams – meaning my first instinct is not to rely on empathy when assessing a situation or hearing of news. I instinctively rely on logic as an analytical person. For me empathy is learned but it is not natural. What that means is I have to be much more purposeful and proactive when it comes to understanding and supporting my team. I must be less judgmental and more forgiving. I need to use tools like Perflo to measure what I would normally not pick up on.

Two themes particularly that I have personally found success from measuring are 'stress' and 'clarity' levels in my teams. I used to think, if people don't tell me, 'Hey Bentzy, I'm feeling stressed' – I assume they are not. If people don't tell me, 'Hey Bentzy, I'm unclear on that task you gave me' – I assume they are clear on it. Of course, this was not only a rookie mistake, but an extremely costly one. Burned out team members leave, and rework costs time and money – both things' startups tend not to have a lot of.

Ironically, in our research and my experience, clarity and stress have a lot to do with one another. Well, to be more precise, lack of clarity, has a lot to do with the stress levels of your team and its members.

Stress

We all know the negative impacts stress can have on employees, and the serious implications for important issues such as team morale, productivity, and turnover rates – which is why understanding its causes is crucial to any manager wishing to achieve success in their team and organization.

Stress doesn't have an impact only on those who feel most affected by it, but also on the team as a whole, so it's important that managers take immediate action and prevent the problem from escalating. Obviously, as mentioned – step 1; Measure stress levels and its causes in your team on a continuous basis.

Measuring stress by asking 'Are you stressed?' or 'How happy are you this week?' grants only surface-level insights that are vague and difficult to act on. What's important is to dig deeper and try to understand the root cause. There may be unique causes of stress for each individual, but there will always be certain shared stressors if something on a team- or project-level is going wrong.

What I've learned the hard way is to never assume that your team is not stressed even if they tell you they aren't, and never force solutions upon them that they haven't requested to address their concerns.

We need to start paying attention to managers' stress.

Monitoring and prioritizing the stress of managers is no less critical for organizations – their stress almost always trickles down to their teams. When a manager is feeling overwhelmed, it's very difficult for them to hide it – and this will be reflected in their team. In our ever-changing world of work, many managers are working more hours than ever before, which adds fuel to the fire.

Clarity

Everything starts with clarity when it comes to team and organizational performance. On the same note, everything can also end without it. Projects often go array due to lack of clarity on tasks, roles, and the overall direction. I'm mad about measuring clarity because it's one of those things that aren't seen or felt. Something almost immeasurable. And that's why it's so crucial to try and get as much of a read on your team's clarity levels in all areas of their work.

Research done by Hay Group across teams that reported to 26,000 managers from 437 different organizations revealed that only 33%[6] of team members felt they had the clarity they needed, and (unsurprisingly) those who felt that they did have clarity performed better, were more willing to take on new challenges, and were less likely to resign. Research by Google had[7] similar results – 'Clarity' was one of the five most important determinants of a team's success.

In larger organizations, clarity 'dilutes' with every step you take down the corporate ladder. This is one of the reasons startups are able to outpace larger, more well-resourced organizations. Startups have less bureaucracy, but they also have a strong sense of purpose and a radical focus instilled in every team member. A greater sense of clarity not only ensures that everyone moves fast, but also that they're moving in the same direction. Granted, it's a lot easier to apply this in a company of ten than in a company of ten thousand, but the principle stands: Executives need to prioritize clarity if they want to be purposeful about organizational effectiveness (Figure 16.3).

Clarity also increases innovation; Researchers have found that the relationship between innovation processes and performance is moderated by goal clarity and commitment: When goal clarity and commitment are high, innovation and performance accelerate one another.

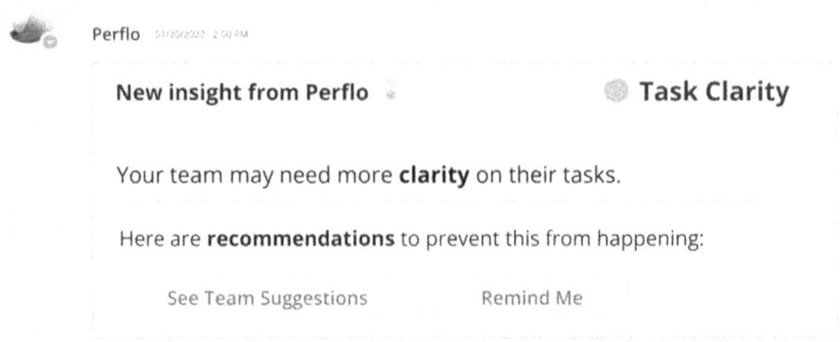

Figure 16.3 Insight – task clarity.

From feedback to action

The next and most important step is to actually do something about it. It's also critical to take action that the team thinks it is a good idea and will help them in the context of their current circumstance – not what the manager thinks is a good idea – there is no one size fits all solution when it comes to stress management for example. Asking the team what would help them to reduce stress and giving them realistic, attainable options that you have the authority to execute is a simple yet very effective way to begin reducing stress in your team.

We've experimented with some success both internally and externally with allowing team members to own the 'feedback to action' process, right from the beginning. We created a framework on a digital collaboration tool for teams to outline what's important to them, what they would do about it, who will be accountable for making sure it happens. This of course creates a strong sense of ownership within the team and builds a culture of continuous improvement – a superior element of high-performing teams.

Many people use external consultants, however with some of the current tools (I won't mention any names) on the market, and the content embedded within them – consultants need to either work alongside these tools or step up their game dramatically to justify the cost of diagnosing and prescribing a team solution.

One of the most pressing topics in the world of employee feedback is how to convert qualitative feedback into practical changes and do it fast enough that it has a positive impact on the item measured. This is where I and others believe, the good research in behavioral science and economics can play a huge part in driving positive change in the workplace in a much more practical and scalable way.

Nudges

Nudges[8] have been used in the consumer world predominantly, both by corporations trying to influence their customers to purchase their products and by governments trying to influence their citizens to make better decisions, impacting social well-being. However, nudges have been underutilized in the workplace, and we're just at the beginning of experimenting with applying the utility of nudging in different areas of the workplace. Nudges can be a super powerful tool when it comes to helping managers lead their teams better. Nudges can also be utilized to help team members make healthier decisions together and collaborate more positively.

Nudges are defined as 'subtle, often subconscious prompts to change people's behavior in a predictable way without forbidding any options or significantly changing their economic incentives'.

Manager nudges are subtle prompts to both alert managers of issues happening in their teams, as well as suggested actions which they can use to approach the issues. Team analytics is the basis, the vehicle for driving nudges. Based on the different pieces of data analyzed, an intelligent system will know when to nudge a manager, and what to alert them of – connecting the dots, and shortening the loop of; feedback to action (Figure 16.4).

Organizations can use nudges for a number of purposes, including, and perhaps one of the best examples – encouraging employees to make healthier choices; by placing healthy snacks next to fattening snacks at lunchtime in office vending machines. This simple action has helped

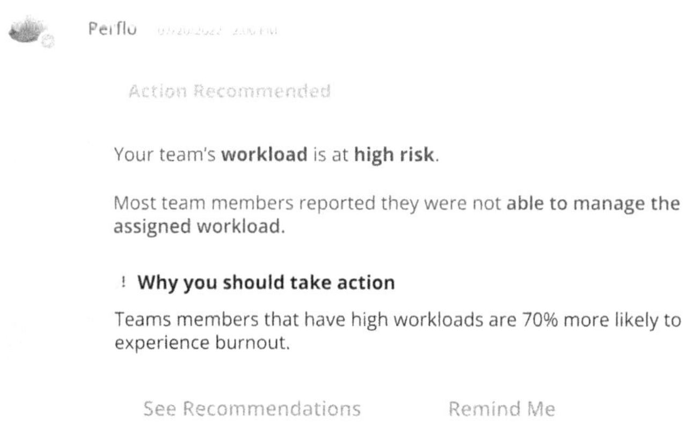

Figure 16.4 Insight – suggestion.

various companies save millions in healthcare costs due to increased focus on health goals (resulting from eating more nutritious foods). Another study showed that nudging employees to save for retirement increased 401(k) contributions by about $22 million per year.[9]

In the business world, nudges are often used in email marketing. For example, if an employee hasn't replied to an email within a certain time frame, the email might be automatically re-sent with a different subject line or font color (or something else that would grab attention).

Nudges can also be effective when it comes to increasing team member productivity. Nudges like helping keep people focused by carving out calendar space for 'focus time', or the use of nudges to help people stay on task and make better decisions. Nudging employees involves using little subtle changes that influence team members toward better work habits.

Some types of nudges that have been tested in the workplace include:

- Placing healthy snacks[10] next to unhealthy snacks in office vending machines.
- Encouraging employees to take a break every hour or so.
- Putting deadlines on tasks to increase focus and productivity.
- Changing the subject line of an email if it hasn't been replied to after a certain time frame.
- Creating charts and graphs for team meetings to help everyone stay on track.

Like I said, I believe we are still in the infancy of the application of behavioral science in the workplace, and nudges will likely be the leading application behind this revolution. There are few technology companies that have properly developed research-backed nudges, and their results speak for themselves. Be wary of those that advertise to use 'nudges' in their products but are in fact using 'notifications' as a dummy.

How team analytics saves projects

When teams fail or under-deliver on a project, there's a tendency to go looking for the reasons in the project plan or the scope. Unfortunately, budgets and timelines are treated as the primary yardstick of success in many project autopsies but analyzing these operational and what I call 'progress-related metrics' rarely yield the answers we need – and if the answers do come, they usually come too late.

An expertly crafted methodology doesn't always translate to project success because methodology won't mean much to a team that's unsure, misaligned, and chronically stressed. This can be troublesome for specifically project managers, who are generally well-versed in things they use to manage projects – processes and methodologies – but not in the ways they can empower people. That's crucial, for obvious reasons: humans deliver projects, methodologies do not. This is not to say that process-related data or project plans are unimportant – of course they are – but these cannot stand alone. If we want to get the full picture of project health, you need to start paying attention to the health of the driving force behind the project – The Team. And that's where team analytics come in.

Notes

1 https://www.mckinsey.com/business-functions/people-and-organizational-performance/our-insights/great-attrition-or-great-attraction-the-choice-is-yours
2 the desire for location flexibility.
3 Another survey.
4 "Positive Workplace Culture: Everything You Need to Know - 6Q." https://inside.6q.io/positive-workplace-culture-everything-you-need-to-know/
"Proof That Positive Work Cultures Are More Productive." 01 Dec. 2015, https://hbr.org/2015/12/proof-that-positive-work-cultures-are-more-productive
5 We will explore this a lot more in Part Two.
6 "New Hay Group Research on Why 1 in 5 Employees is Headed for the Door." https://www.hr.com/en/communities/new-hay-group-research-on-why-1-in-5-employees-is-_h50ze7a1.html
7 What is Project Aristotle? – Institute Success.
8 What is a Nudge? – NudgeU - Weblogs at Harvard.
9 ""Nudging" Employees May Improve Retirement Savings." 08 Sept. 2017, https://401ktv.com/retirement-savings-nudge-employees/
10 "15 Examples of Workplace Nudging – HR Trend Institute." 09 Nov. 2020, https://hrtrendinstitute.com/2020/11/09/15-examples-of-workplace-nudging/

17 Leveraging AI for team effectiveness

In the very near future AI will be a normal part of everyone's day-to-day lives.[1] Just as we use data to help us make decisions now, AI will be influencing the majority of the decisions we think we are making, like what we eat, how we entertain ourselves, and even who we date. While some may see this as a scary future, it's important to remember that AI is just a tool – and one that can be used for good or bad depending on how we choose to use it.

Organizations use AI in every part of their business such as marketing, customer service, and finance. Businesses have started using AI for tasks such as lead generation and social media monitoring.[2] They use AI to create predictive models to identify which customers are likely to churn or buy certain products. However, there is a huge lacking in the people department of the organization. Not just to predict things like attrition, but to help teams run smoother, and help managers empower them better (and faster).

Using AI in our personal lives

AI is being used to help us stay healthy and fit. Wearable devices that track our activity levels, heart rate, and sleep patterns[3] will become more commonplace, and they'll be able to give us custom recommendations on how to live a healthier life. We'll also see a rise in the number of virtual health assistants, which can provide us with personalized advice on everything from diet and exercise to mental health and stress management.

Another way AI will impact our lives by helping us make better decisions, by getting real-time feedback on our choices. For example, if you're trying to decide between two restaurants, you could use an app that would consider your previous food preferences and tell you which one is more likely to give you a better experience.

AI will make us more productive by automating tasks that are currently time-consuming or difficult to do. For instance, you might use an AI-powered assistant to book your travel plans based on different variables, both conscious and contextual. Or you might use a tool that helps you automatically file your expenses or keep track of your to-do list.

DOI: 10.4324/9781003177753-17

Using AI in our work lives

AI also has and can have a big impact on our work lives. We'll see more tools that help us automate repetitive tasks, freeing up our time to focus on more important things. For instance, if you're a customer service representative, you might use an AI-powered chatbot to handle simple questions from customers, leaving you with more time to deal with complex issues and/or relationship building.

We'll already see AI being used more for decision-making in the workplace. Forward-thinking organizations use AI-powered analytics to make better decisions about everything from marketing strategies to product development. And we'll see a rise in the use of virtual assistants in the workplace, which can help us with everything from scheduling meetings to booking travel plans.

But still there is a vastly untapped world of possibility that needs to be explored in our work life. There is huge opportunity to leverage AI to improve our life at work, particularly within the realm of the 'team experience'. How we operate, make decisions, and problem solve as a collective. In addition to making our lives more efficient and productive, these advancements will help us to build more human relationships and open time and space for more creative collaboration and innovation. It will ensure people are matched on the projects that they are most keen on working on, and the tasks that are most suitable to their skillset and career goals.

Organizations already use things like Natural Language Processing[4] (NLP) to gauge employee sentiment from the annual survey or use AI to screen job candidates faster, but that's old news. What I'm talking about here is incorporating the positive attributes of machine learning to power the day-to-day of an employee's life. A team's life. A manager's life. How much is being invested in improving their lives and experience at work.

Time and time again we hear organizations proclaiming their people as their 'number one asset' – but if we take a closer look at the way that technologies and processes are being utilized in organizations it would suggest otherwise. The priority is to use these tools for increasing efficiency and cost savings, and not people empowerment. To future-proof our organizations and position them for success in an ever-changing world, we need to truly start putting our people first – and that means using tools and resources like AI to help us help them.

The future of AI is bright, and it holds a lot of promise for both our personal and professional lives. With the right safeguards in place, there's no reason why AI can't be a force for good in our world.

Further on we will look at how AI can be incorporated into projects and increase the likelihood of project success.

Why now?

In one sentence – you can't manage teams in the new world of work, the same way you managed them in the old world of work. Whatever that may mean to you – virtual collaboration, business pivots, or simply the current sense of uncertainty. Change brings about the need for new ways of doing things, and in order to stay ahead and build future-proof organizations – we cannot rely on our old ways of doing things.

When teams go virtual managers have less visibility and the risk of misalignment and disengagement increases dramatically – thus the need for real-time data on engagement-related factors is critical for team success.

The great resignation – employees leave teams and managers, not companies. Monitoring the proven reasons why employees leave in order to prevent the levels of attrition we are seeing is now a top business imperative.

Agility is no longer a nice to have – to be adaptable and continuously iterate products and business models, you need to be able to spot issues in real-time and be proactive when running projects.

Servant Leadership – 'soft skills and empathy are cited as the most critical skills of top leaders today[5] – this starts with understanding your team and where you can support them.

Positively, there is a new-found appreciation for the need to be people-first when running a company. The growing, and now painful realization that putting people first is a business imperative, will only fuel the need for concepts like team analytics. It covers the essentially of putting these principles to practice, listening, understanding, and prioritizing their needs and feedback of your people, teams, and organization.

Notes

1 One of the authors of this book has explored the impact of AI on project management in another Routledge book 'AI and the Project Manager: How the Rise of Artificial Intelligence Will Change Your World'.
2 "Artificial Intelligence in Business: 10 Notable Examples." https://onlinedegrees.sandiego.edu/artificial-intelligence-business/
3 "How AI Enabled Wearables are Changing Healthcare and … - eInfochips." 11 Dec. 2019, https://www.einfochips.com/blog/how-ai-enabled-wearables-are-changing-healthcare-and-fitness-industry/
4 "What is Natural Language Processing? | IBM." 02 Jul. 2020, https://www.ibm.com/cloud/learn/natural-language-processing.
5 Empathy Is The Most Important Leadership Skill According ...

18 Long-term business benefits

I think it's now clear what the benefits are on the manager and team level. I'd like to add that the benefits to using team analytics within your organization extend long beyond the lifecycle of a single team. As more and more teams implement the continuous feedback and analysis process, the more your organization 'learns'. It's a system very similar to that of compound interest. An improved understanding of what makes a great team great, and what is influencing the success or failure of your projects, ultimately lead to higher success rates if those learnings are applied properly. Imagine running a continuous internal experiment within your organization while you sleep. This is the power of data, machine learning, and organizational psychology – all working in unison. You won't need a big management consulting firm to come in and dissect problems, only to provide you with multi-million-dollar PowerPoints.

Once the data scientists and business analysts want to start getting involved, you know you've got some valuable insights they'd love to get their hands on. And you should let them. Correlations and regression analysis will prove to be a powerful force in identifying what makes your teams tick, and what your organization can do to improve and reach optimal levels of productivity and team satisfaction. Get creative, look at external events, financial results, any other variables that you may think aren't an influencing factor. Perhaps certain projects are more effective in the summer rather than the wintertime. Who knows, I bet you never included weather data in your analysis though!

DOI: 10.4324/9781003177753-18

19 Conclusion

I want to take this opportunity to really push forward that, the ideas covered in this book, and the impact we promise team analytics can have does not refer to a survey or health check process your team may already have or may now decide to implement. Team analytics is more than just a continuous feedback and analysis process. It is a management framework for building and leading successful team-based organizations based on a science whichleveragesdata as the foundation for continuous team improvement.

I say this because I fear that an individual may go back to their organization and do an assessment or run some surveys and hope for drastic change. This requires a mindset shift, particularly for the non-people-centric leader, and a process shift for the leader that already values its importance. The effort of this transition is minuscule in comparison to the returns it will bring. I wish you the best of luck.

Now, without further a due – I will humbly shut up, and let you learn from someone who not only has the experience and wisdom to deliver this message, but who puts his money where his mouth is, and drives change daily, in organizations that he is both part of and those he advises - Sir Peter Taylor.[1]

Note

1 Sir Peter Taylor (not yet endorsed by His Majesty).

DOI: 10.4324/9781003177753-19

20 Part 2: Projects

In Part 2 Peter Taylor (aka The Lazy Project Manager) extends the conversation started by Bentzy Goldman to consider how we can apply these principles of team performance to projects and the real need for this approach in the project world. To also explore the reality that projects are still about people first and foremost, and that team performance in the project world has a completely different dynamic than other teams. Before exploring how this can be improved, significantly improved, through a focus on team behaviour, sentiment, and dynamics.

DOI: 10.4324/9781003177753-20

21 Why projects (still) aren't successful

Big projects fail at an astonishing rate. Whether major technology installations, post-merger integrations, or new growth strategies, these efforts consume tremendous resources over months or even years. Yet as study after study has shown, they frequently deliver disappointing returns—by some estimates, in fact, well over half the time. And the toll they take is not just financial. These failures demoralize employees who have laboured diligently to complete their share of the work. Declares Nadim Matta and Ron Ashkenas in an article 'Why Good Projects Fail Anyway[1]' (Harvard Business Review)

Consider the following scary facts[2]:

- Only 64% of projects meet their goals
- 70% of companies report having at least one failed project in the last year
- Organizations lose $109 million for every $1 billion invested in projects and programs
- High-performing organisations successfully complete 89% of projects, while low performers only complete 36% successfully. Low performers waste nearly 12 times more resources than high-performing organizations
- Only one-third of companies always prepare a business case for new projects

Look, you can troll the world wide web of wonder and find hundreds of gleeful articles telling us all how we, the project world, are failing but the reality is that we deliver some truly amazing results. Doubt this? Then just look around at some of the amazing construction projects on your nearby horizon, consider the achievements in the recent pandemic in the production of vaccines and equipment at astonishing speed, note the rapid acceleration (literally in some cases) of the e-motor generation of vehicles now common on our roads.

In one of my keynotes, I joke about this and put up a slide that shows two numbers. The first is how many hits you get when you search for 'Sad Project Manager' – today I got 57.5 million (it will change with every

DOI: 10.4324/9781003177753-21

search of course). Holy batman you might say, we are one truly miserable bunch out there and maybe that is because most projects are failing.

But put in the counter search for 'Happy Project Manager' and you will see the comparison – today it was 227 million hits, so hey, life is good, and we are doing great things.

We are also living in a complex world that is getting more complex and moving faster – one of the author's explores this in their book 'Make Your Business Agile: A Roadmap for Transforming Your Management and Adapting to the New Normal'.[3]

The point here is that projects are challenging, and it is not the method, the process, the communication plan, the issue and risk logs, the escalation path or any of that that makes the real difference between success and failure. It is the people.

Think about it. At the end of any project have you ever heard people thanking the methodology[4]? The governance? The reporting procedure? The risk strategy or the communication plan? No. They thank the 'people'. Simple as that.

Projects are about people, and they always will be.[5]

If you buy in to that statement (and you really should) then how can we make projects better? How can we make them even more successful? How can we make people deliver amazing project success?

Well, it all goes back to the team.

The collective group of individuals that come together and prove that together they are more than they are apart.

'A Whole is Greater Than the Sum of Its Parts'

First allegedly coined by the philosopher Aristotle,[6] this phrase aptly defines the modern concept of collaboration and synergy. It also echoes the T.E.A.M. acronym – together, everyone achieves more.[7] (Which is the motto of my own PMO coincidently.)

So, let's explore how everyone together can achieve more.

Notes

1 https://hbr.org/2003/09/why-good-projects-fail-anyway
2 Key project management statistics gathered by Wrike. The statistics are based on figures from the US, but still provide some important lessons when it comes to the global project management approach by leading organizations.
3 Make Your Business Agile: A Roadmap for Transforming Your Management and Adapting to the 'New Normal' (Routledge).
4 And I don't really care about whether you are old school waterfall, modern time agile, or anything and everything in between – it is still about the people.
5 In 'AI and the Project Manager: How the Rise of Artificial Intelligence Will Change Your World' (Routledge) Taylor explores the rapidly impacting world of Artificial Intelligence on projects and project managers, but concludes that projects are still about people in the end.

6 Aristotle, Metaphysics – what was written was 'For however many things have a plurality of parts and are not merely a complete aggregate but instead some kind of a whole beyond its parts …'

7 The alternative to this is 'Together Everyone Annoys Me' but I really don't subscribe to that version.

22 The missing phase of Tuckman's model of team development

Long ago, Bruce Tuckman[1] defined the stages of teams as 'storming, forming and norming' (and now 'mourning' as well, as project teams disband quickly and move on to other projects and other teams).

These have, and continue, to work well in the team formation and dynamics space, and, I believe, are wholly relevant to today's teams (as they were back in the 1960s when Tuckman formulated his model).

Not that there aren't many other models covering this area:

- Group dynamics (Lewin[2]) which considers how people interact and the common perceptions that arise within a group community
- Psychoanalysis (Bion[3]) which is concerned with the natural and common defensive behaviors of team members
- FIRO/Human Elements (Schutz[4]) which considers the compatibility between people using behaviours of inclusion, control, openness, and how those behaviours relate to feelings of significance, competence, and likeability
- Team Roles such as MTR-i or Belbin[5] examine how team performance is related to psychological roles taken by different team members
- Personality type theories, such as Myers Briggs,[6] Disc,[7] consider how the different preferences of team members affect their interactions in-between team members, and therefore, team performance
- Team Islands[8] and In/Out groups,[9] showing how sub-teams can form as a result of members having different characteristics or being separated by a geographical boundary

But personally, thinking about the formation of a new team and the likely path that this team will progress (hopefully on the road to productivity and high performance) Tuckman's model stands the test of time.

At least it does with some slight adaptation for the world of projects.

As noted in the article 'Using the Stages of Team Development'[10] by Judith Stein (MIT[11])

DOI: 10.4324/9781003177753-22

The most commonly used framework for a team's stages of development was developed in the mid-1960s by Bruce W. Tuckman. Although many authors have written variations and enhancements to Tuckman's work, his descriptions of Forming, Storming, Norming and Performing provide a useful framework for looking at your own team.

Each stage of team development has its own recognizable feelings and behaviours; understanding why things are happening in certain ways on your team can be an important part of the self-evaluation process.

The four stages are a helpful framework for recognizing a team's behavioural patterns; they are most useful as a basis for team conversation, rather than boxing the team into a "diagnosis." And just as human development is not always linear (think of the five-year old child who reverts to thumb-sucking when a new sibling is born), team development is not always a linear process. Having a way to identify and understand causes for changes in the team behaviours can help the team maximize its process and its productivity.

The original fantastic four

Simply summarized the (original) four stages are:

1 Forming
This is all about the first gathering of the team members and during this stage they tend to think and behave independently – which is not surprising at this point since they are no automatic guidelines for them to do otherwise.

Starting with a team building process the focus then is on introductions, agreement of goals and responsibilities (typically as allocated by the project manager). Most likely with regular reinforcement and explanation of these goals as team members connect, engage, and develop.

The team tends to be led at this stage and may well be relatively uninformed of the issues and objectives of the team. The individual members may well be motivated but probably not motivated by interaction and collaboration with the other team members at this point.

Mature team members begin to model appropriate behaviour even at this early phase, and all team members are usually on their best behaviour but very focused on themselves rather than the collective.

The major task functions typically concern orientation, and here members will begin to try and find their place and become orientated, but this is also the stage in which group members test boundaries, create ground rules, and define organizational standards.

The project or team leader focuses on scoping the tasks, aiming to achieve agreement on the approach that will be taken, the method that will be followed, the governance that will be in place, and the overall vision.

Concerns will no doubt be expressed, and opinions shared.

To move on, or grow, from this stage to the next, each member must relinquish the comfort of non-threatening topics and risk the possibility of conflict.

2 Storming

The second stage is where the 'rubber hits the road' as it were with team members initiating the working together.

The group starts to sort itself out and to begin to (hopefully) gain each other's trust.

But first, before this trust is achieved, individuals voice their personal opinions, and conflict may arise between some team members as power and status are both fought for and assigned.

Previous perceived status from other work is considered by each team member, position in relation to other team members is deemed precious, and hierarchy is all.

Team members need to discover each other's individual working styles and what it is like to work with each other as one team; it also identifies the hierarchy of positions in the group.

Feelings and emotions can be very mixed at this stage. There is often a positive and almost polite atmosphere, where people are pleasant to each other, and feel a mixture of excitement, eagerness, and positiveness. But others may have feelings of suspicion, fear, and anxiety and perhaps feel threatened by other team members.

The more common this is amongst the team the more 'storming' occurs.

These feelings can also include the team leader, where participants question the actions or decision of the leader as the workload and demands increase or become clearer in definition.

This phase can become destructive to the team and will lower motivation if allowed to get out of control, and the role of the team leader is to allow the 'storming' to happen, and not supress it for later on, but guide the individuals towards the third stage of 'norming'.

Tolerance between team members and the acceptance of their inevitable differences must be emphasised because without such tolerance and patience the team will fail.

It is normal that tension, struggle, and sometimes arguments occur, and. For some, this stage can be uncomfortable, but teams will find a way through this as long as the leader 'leads' well and the visibility of purpose of the team goal is well defined and valued by all.

3 Norming

Resolved disagreements and personality clashes result in greater intimacy, and an increased spirit of co-operation.

In this third stage, all team members begin to take responsibility for the success of the team's goals. They start tolerating other team members, accepting them for who they are, and how they work.

The team is 'norming'.

But the danger here is that members may be so focused on preventing conflict that they are reluctant to share controversial ideas.

4 Performing

With group norms and roles now fully established, and team members working with a significant degree of trust and open collaboration, the team collectively can often reach an unexpectedly high level of success.

By this time, they are motivated and knowledgeable, they are now competent, autonomous, and able to handle the decision-making process without supervision. Dissent is expected and allowed as long as it is channelled through means acceptable to the team.

Leaders of the team during this phase are almost always participating, but the team will make most of the necessary decisions themselves.

And then there were the famous five

5 Adjourning

Tuckman later included a fifth stage – Adjourning (or some refer to it as 'Mourning') considering the feeling of loss perhaps at the end of a high-performing period of impactful work with a great collaborative team – I have often seen 'old' teams regathering over coffee or lunch or on a call to keep connected to their previous team members).

After being invited by Group and Organizational Studies to publish and update his original model, Tuckman, with Mary Ann Jensen, revisited and reviewed the literature. They concluded that an important step in the small group life cycle was this 'fifth' stage of ultimate separation which occurred at the end of the cycle.

Life beyond the temporary

It is argued that a team that lasts may transcend to a 'transforming' phase of achievement.

Such 'Transformational management' can produce major changes in performance through synergy and is more far-reaching than transactional management.

And it didn't stop there either.

Timothy Biggs suggested that an additional stage be added of 'norming' after 'forming' and renaming the traditional norming stage 're-norming'. This addition is designed to reflect that there is a period after forming where the performance of a team gradually improves, and the interference of a leader who is content with that level of performance will prevent a team from progressing through the storming stage to true performance. This puts the emphasis back on the team and leader, as the storming stage must be actively engaged in order to succeed – too many 'diplomats' or 'peacemakers', especially in a leadership role, may prevent the team from reaching their full potential.

So, in reality, to get through to high team performance the advice seems to be, let the inevitable happen and don't interfere (too much anyway).

It keeps coming.

Rickards and Moger[12] proposed a similar extension to the Tuckman model when a group breaks out of its norms, through a process of creative problem-solving.

OK I think that this is more than enough, and I want to go back to the simpler, original concept of the four main stages – Forming, storming, norming, and performing. I feel that we will all recognize these, certainly if you have ever led a newly formed team.

It is within these that I have seen the variation that applies to temporary teams, such as project teams, with a variable application and attendance of team members over a period of time.

Adding the essential sixth sense

6 Disrupting

Based on this many times over observed phenomena, I am going to boldly declare yet another stage to the famous Tuckman model.

Not a sequential stage, but a stage that overlays and impacts the first four (original) phases of teamwork and performance levels.

It is most seen in the 'Norming' and 'Performing' stages and is most impactful in the 'Performing' phase due to potential disruption of the overall team dynamics and therefore, performance levels.

Hence the naming of 'Disrupting' stage.

Notes

1 Bruce Tuckman was an American Psychological Researcher who carried out his research into the theory of group dynamics. In 1965, he published a theory known as 'Tuckman's stages of group development'. According to this theory, there are four phases of group development: Forming, Storming, Norming, Performing.
2 The social psychologist Kurt Lewin coined the term group dynamics to describe the positive and negative forces within groups of people. In 1945, he established The Group Dynamics Research Center at the Massachusetts Institute of Technology, the first institute devoted explicitly to the study of group dynamics.
3 Wilfred Bion was an influential English psychoanalyst, who became president of the British Psychoanalytical Society, he specifically identified three basic assumptions: dependency, fight-flight, and pairing. When a group adopts any one of these basic assumptions, it interferes with the task the group is attempting to accomplish.
4 In 1958, Dr. Will Schutz formally introduced a theory of interpersonal relations called FIRO (Fundamental Interpersonal Relations Orientation). The theory presented three dimensions of interpersonal relations posited to be necessary and sufficient to explain most human interactions.

5 The Belbin Team Inventory, also called Belbin Self-Perception Inventory or Belbin Team Role Inventory, is a behavioural test. It was devised by Raymond Belbin to measure preference for nine Team Roles.
6 The Belbin Team Inventory, also called Belbin Self-Perception Inventory or Belbin Team Role Inventory, is a behavioural test. It was devised by Raymond Meredith Belbin to measure preference for nine Team Roles.
7 DISC assessments are behaviour self-assessment tools based on the 1928 DISC emotional and behavioural theory of psychologist William Moulton Marston. The tools are designed to predict job performance.
8 The phenomenon of 'Team Islands' refers to the status of teams in the workplace, and occurs when: small teams work well together, but there are problems in the relationships between those teams.
9 When working with teams, we often hear people complain that there seems to be an 'in' group and an 'out' group. The team leader has 'favourites', or in a cross-functional team one sub-group seems to have more influence with decision makers than others.
10 https://hr.mit.edu/learning-topics/teams/articles/stages-development
11 https://www.mit.edu/ Massachusetts Institute of Technology
12 'Creative Leadership Processes in Project Team Development: An Alternative to Tuckman's Stage Model' by Tudor Rickards and Susan Moger.

23 Why project teams are simply different to other teams

Let's consider the world of the temporary endeavor, the world of change delivery, the world where teams get together to align to a common goal but do not become a permanent community, and one where they quite possibly are still undertaking their day job and being part of a 'permanent' team (Figure 23.1).

And that is the key difference number 1.

A project team will, most likely, incorporate team members who are not 100% dedicated to the project and the project team members. They will, instead, be part-time contributors (and not always voluntary ones at that) who, in parallel to the project work, must maintain their own 'business as usual', and keep on supporting their full-time/permanent team colleagues.

Difference number 2 is that project teams are never all gathered on day one and you get to keep them for the duration of the project. At least, that has never happened in my experience – it probably does on some exceptional basis, but it is not the normality. The reason is simply economics, businesses cannot afford to dedicate valuable resources in this way, nor can they afford to backfill 'lost' team members whilst they are working on a project.

Instead, team members come and go, appearing when they are specifically needed – or their skills are – and then disappearing as soon as that piece of work is completed.

As such, whilst perhaps the core team has cracked on with the whole forming, storming, norming process – maybe even heading toward the performing level – these part-timers appear as and when needed and are not necessarily at the same status as the core team. The project team could be all 'norming' when new a resource, or resources appear and drift the whole team back on to the storming phase. Not intentionally, not maliciously, not with project sabotage in mind but simply because they have arrived fresh and now need to find their place in the overall team.

Difference number 3 brings us in to the world of internal and external teams trying to find a way to work together in a rapid way. Again, cost is typically the reason here. Start using a resource (especially an external expensive resource) and the budget starts getting burned up. Burn too much

DOI: 10.4324/9781003177753-23

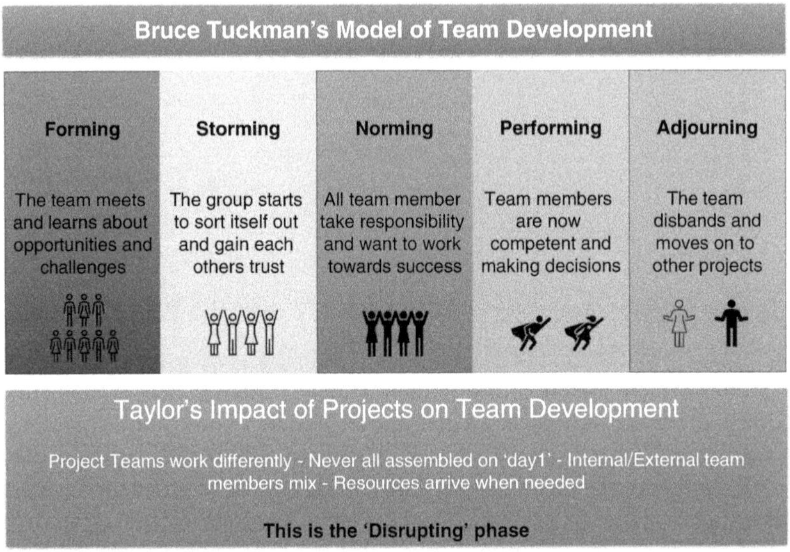

Figure 23.1 Tuckman's model of development.

on just 'getting to know each other' and bang, your project is overrunning on expenditure, and you are already in trouble as a project manager, and the project has barely even started.

And if you think about it, internal teams do have one thing in common – the culture of the organization that they work for. External resources will bring into the mix their own culture, expectations, biases, and so on. It all adds into the mix of potential 'storming' igniting elements.

And finally, difference number 4. Objectives, or rather varying objectives that might not align to your project goals and expected outcomes.

Think of it this way. You are a skilled subject matter expert (SME) and you are part of a team of internal experts overseeing 'x'. This is your primary focus and the one that your manager will measure you on. Because of your expert level knowledge, you are assigned to project 'y' to offer up advice at the project start and again toward the end of the project build phase. And because, once again, you are a star within your team and the company, you are also offered out to project 'z' for a few hours to help as needed.

Where is your objective alignment? How will you deal with the conflicting demand on your time? And, since you are only engaged with project 'y' and project 'z' on an occasional basis, how will you interact with the existing core teams on both these projects?

You can hardly expect to seamlessly join a performing team without having some impact – which could range from minimal to significant impact, especially if there is an issue I have found.

All these differences will have a disrupting impact on the project team dynamics and, as such, projects just are different. The project manager cannot build their team once and guide them (without excessive intervention) through the storming to norming stages before the team naturally progresses to 'performing'. They can't do this because resources are constantly joining and leaving the project. It is all part of the resource plan to ensure the balance between having the right people with the right skills in place at the right time and not wasting people's time, or the cost associated with their time.

Let me give one example of this.

On a project I led some years ago there was a great core team. We connected well, the vision of the project was understood by all, and the project was progressing to plan. Happy days.

There was a need for specific SME to join the project for three key points of work. All short-term and all several weeks apart.

The SME was brilliant but, shall we say, somewhat different in their outlook on life and personal filters.

The result of this was that after the first round of engagement by this person my core team were unhappy with the way they were spoken to, talked down to, and generally challenged, with their efforts ridiculed by the SME.

Now to be fair, the SMEs comments and guidance were not out of order, in fact they were correct in what had to be changed on this project's deliverables but, the way they were delivered was unpalatable and disruptive.

After calming the team down and them returning to one big happy family the time came for the SME to re-join the team for a few days and all hell broke loose within hours.

The team spiralled into a brand-new storming phase faster than you could say 'Bruce Tuckman' and it took a lot of my time, to calm the rough seas once again.

And guess what? The third time the SME was due to contribute to our project the storming took place even before the SME turned up.

Sometimes you can't swap out people to suit your needs, or that of your team, so you must manage the team dynamics as best you can and understanding that projects are different is a great place to start.

Tuckman does recognize this but doesn't specifically consider this as significant as I do.

Even the most high-performing teams will revert to earlier stages in certain circumstances. Many long-standing teams go through these cycles many times as they react to changing circumstances. For example, a change in leadership may cause the team to revert to storming as the new people challenge the existing norms and dynamics of the team.

And in case you were wondering about it, yes there is a concept of 'swarming'[1] but I am not going to specifically talk about that.

Nor am I heading in the direction of the yawning[2] concept.

Notes

1 Swarming – In agile software development, high-performance teams will exhibit a swarm behavior as they come together, collaborate, and focus on solving a single problem.
2 A lot of management trainers add an extra phase beyond performing: 'yawning'. This recognizes that a team, once formed and into performing stage, can become stale. It is a teaching aid as much as an extension of the Tuckman model, to highlight the importance for a team leader to keep the team fresh and challenged – in both the task and relationships dimensions – if you are to maintain high performance. It is also a reminder that, if your team slips from its high-performance levels, this may be what is happening.

24 It's all gone virtual

And then we all went remote.

In fact, we were heading into an increasingly remote project world already, before the pandemic, but then we went totally remote for a significant period.

Which was interesting. Back in the financial recession of 2008/9 it was quickly obvious that commencing projects completely remotely was not being successful. Whilst cancelling face-to-face meetings was a critical cost-saving exercise the lack of connection between team members had its impact and project struggled. It wasn't until we re-invested in at least some physical meetings for the key team members that we saw projects stabilize and proceed toward success.

In the recent couple of years this is very different. Technology (and people) were better prepared to engage and work collectively for a common purpose.

There is a move, now that some degree of normality returns, to a hybrid world but still we all must think, and act, slightly differently to lead our project teams.

Deloitte[1] stated in the article 'Resilient Work – Transform work, the workforce, and the workplace',

> *The pandemic tested the flexibility and responsiveness of work and culture everywhere. It accelerated resilient organizations towards their future goals but tested the rest to breaking point.*
>
> *Organizations everywhere have experienced unprecedented disruption caused by the pandemic over the past year or so. For those without the resilience to adapt and ride the waves of change it has felt like anything from a white-knuckle ride to a full-blown shipwreck. The vital lesson we have all learned it is that we can no longer delay our reimagining and restructuring of the way we do work.*

I believe that, in the project world, we as a global community have reimagined and delivered on that reimagining in a phenomenal way.

About hybrid (project) working it is worth checking out the PMI[2] LIVE Continuous Improvement for Hybrid Working video by Damion Albinson and Rich Seddon.

DOI: 10.4324/9781003177753-24

> *For many of us, being part of a hybrid working structure where our teams are spread across different countries, different sites, or working remotely, is now a reality. Effective hybrid team collaboration is a requirement of this way of working, and even more so as an improvement practitioner, where mastering the art of facilitating a hybrid team is imperative to achieving great outcomes for your improvement actions and projects.*

But what's different about running project teams remotely (either completely virtual or in a hybrid manner)?

Long ago, as we have already discussed, Bruce Tuckman defined the stages of teams as 'storming, forming and norming' (and now 'mourning' as well as project teams disband quickly and move on to other projects and other teams).

In my personal view virtual teams tend to get past the 'forming' stage quickly, as teams always have. Resources are identified and roles defined.

It starts getting tricky just after that.

The 'storming' phase is important in preparing the team for working together, resolving character imbalances, sorting out territorial issues, and generally getting everyone to know everyone else. Now without a face-to-face session (or two … or three) this will be very challenging, and so you have to compensate somehow. During this time decisions don't come easily within the group, and team members will no doubt vie for position as they attempt to establish themselves in relation to other team members. Clarity of purpose increases, but plenty of uncertainties will persist. Typically cliques and factions form, and there may be power struggles. The team needs to be focused on its goals to avoid becoming distracted by relationships and emotional issues. Compromises may well be required to enable real progress.

So what? How does this change the role of the manager?

In a virtual situation a lot of these issues can be hidden, so as the leader you almost must force the matter. It's also very easy to jump to a wrong conclusion about a fellow team member, apply stereotypical attributes, and miss tensions hidden by a reduced communication process and lack of physical visibility as to how people are behaving.

If possible, make the investment in a 'hothouse' face-to-face meeting. By this I mean an intensive, almost 24/7 multi-day team experience. Use an external facilitator to drive the storming process harder and faster to a conclusion. Make the business case that this is an investment, no matter how significant, that will pay off.

And by 24/7, I mean not just work but social activities as well, dinners with the team members, activities that bring people together and that are fun and visits to local sights and events.

At dinners why not let the team organize the evening plans, what food do they enjoy, where is best to go, logistics of travel – don't organize everything for them, let them work together and learn in simple ways.

Based in the individual's personal ambitions and likes you can bond with the group by agreeing goals for each team member that the group can follow, maybe to lose a little weight, or train for a sporting event, or visit somewhere special, or write an article for a magazine – it doesn't matter what it is just that the team have some insight in to each other's lives.

If this is financially and/or logistically impossible, then you may just have to accept that the 'storming' phase will be longer than usual.

What is your role once things are up and running: the period that should require less of your time as manager?

Once you hit 'norming' the challenges decrease to a degree, but you must be able to maintain the team spirit. At this time there should be agreement and consensus amongst the team members.

Their roles and responsibilities should be clear and accepted with the larger decisions made by group agreement and you as the leader should facilitate and enable all of this.

Commitment and unity should be strong. This is also a time when the team may engage in fun and social activities perhaps based in the challenges that you agreed during the face-to-face meeting earlier on.

So, what do you do when you can't just head off to the pub for a beer or two?

One technique I have used is the 'It's Friday' email exchange. On a Friday, it is encouraged that all those funnies, Dilbert cartoons, YouTube videos, and so on are shared amongst the team. Be careful though – err on the side of caution of what is funny to whom; culture, sex, and beliefs can vary a huge amount in a team.

Another technique is to explore what you don't know about the team members. Each week on the team calls, get one or two to share hobbies or something unusual that they do outside of work hours. Making new connections with common hobbies helps bond a team.

And finally, rotate the team calls. Don't take the lead each time yourself, hand it over to a team member to take 20 minutes or so to share what they have personally been doing in the past week, there is nothing worse than a conference call that is just a one-way piece of communication, and you wonder if anyone is listening. By allowing the team members to 'own' the call and to regularly lead the call then their interest and interaction should increase significantly.

And then on to 'performing' – when the team is more strategically aware and knows clearly why it is doing through a shared vision. It can stand on its own feet with no interference or participation from the leader. There is a focus on over-achieving goals, and the team makes most of the decisions against criteria agreed with the leader.

Make it to this stage and the challenges of remote working will have pretty much disappeared or the team will resolve the issues themselves and you will wonder what all the fuss was at the beginning.

And it's not all over yet.

Tuckman's fifth stage 'adjourning[3]' refers to the break-up of the group, a point in time when hopefully the project is completed successfully.

Everyone can move on to new things feeling good about what's been achieved.

From an organizational perspective, recognition of and sensitivity to people's vulnerabilities in Tuckman's fifth stage is helpful, particularly if members of the group have been closely bonded and feel a sense of insecurity or threat from this change.

Well, you do need to deal with the 'mourning' aspect and perhaps a way of doing this is by keeping in touch with the team as they move on to new challenges and move through this new period of change. Social media is a great way to do this and allows for a close network of support amongst the team as they progress onwards; and who knows, you may all meet up sometime in the future on another new project.

Certainly, the lessons learned in successfully working with a virtual team should be carried by the virtual team members on to their next projects.

And then there is the sixth 'stage' that I have already positioned, that of 'disrupting'.

In a virtual world the disruption that will inevitably occur will most likely be less immediately obvious but just as impactful. The virtual team leader will have to be on the ball and ready to deal with team instability that may well occur as new team members join and depart throughout the project lifecycle.

Notes

1 https://www2.deloitte.com/global/en/covid-19/resilient-work.html?id=uk:2ps:3gl:4resilience(resilienthub,_resilient_orgaization):GC1000014:6abt:20211001:gcp100039_3
2 https://pmi.co.uk/knowledge-hub/continuous-improvement-for-hybrid-working/
3 Or 'Mourning' as some prefer.

25 Creative teaming, when two different worlds collide

Our thanks to Dr. Paul Thomason[1] for his contribution to the idea of bridging the two worlds that are now our reality in a work environment.

An interesting notion

Occasionally, an interesting and amusing notion crosses the mind. What if you were to introduce one set of friends (from one area of your life, say the workplace), to this other group of friends (let's say from college or school). I'd be willing to bet that many of us just shrug off that notion as simply ludicrous. (Imagine if either one of these groups started to realize what you're really like when you let your hair down!) Now imagine something similar in a workplace setting where two very different teams come together (think Mars and Jupiter are different), and you'll be on target for a project experience I had a few years ago.

To set the context, the stakes couldn't have been higher. Two major contractors had attempted the state-wide consolidation of all state agency infrastructure into a single data center operating under the service management model of the ITIL framework. This meant pulling all the IT functions of 28 state agencies into a single physical entity, with all systems, processes, and technical activities managed centrally by a team of highly competent subject matter experts and their respective teams, under a highly prescriptive service delivery model. Imagine this as white glove premium 24/7 customer IT support.

I was contracted as the lead Program Manager into what was known as a Multi-Source Integrator (MSI) PMO. This meant that the State had contracted with one company, whose job was to pull together and manage several other companies to build out the entire solution. As the MSI PMO, myself, and a team of program managers had to stand-up the entire operation in six months and pass off the operational running of the enterprise to the operations team at that time. To do that, the company I was hired into brought in some very high-ranking subject matter experts – all leaders in their respective fields, to set everything up. The office feeling was very stoic and incredibly formal given the high stakes of the engagement, largely due to the client being across the street and frequent excursions for meetings.

DOI: 10.4324/9781003177753-25

In addition to building out my team of program managers to help pull this work together, I also had a set of deliverables for which I was responsible. One of these was the Service Management Manual (SMM). This didn't seem too daunting until I realized what this is. The SMM is an online document that outlines in painful detail, how every process, procedure, and step-by-step mechanism should be deployed. From how to respond to a disaster recovery incident, to updating the Hardware Inventory database (CMBD) whenever a new server or hard disk is deployed in the data center, and as far reaching as the security protocols for onboarding staff into the data center itself. A lot of detail and, as it turns out, over 1500 documents in total. Oh, and the deadline for this was three months, not six.

I needed a team of technical writers to help pull these documents together to ensure the same tone of voice was consistent throughout the SMM, and the technical layout was formatted correctly for each section of the manual. So, I began the process of scanning resumes, interviewing, and subsequently hiring my technical writing team. There were very eclectic candidates with wide-ranging experience, none of course directly relevant to what I needed, so it was going to be a best fit and gut-feel approach to hiring.

I interviewed a handful of candidates for two roles. With experienced candidates comes a level of maturity, and each had a very interesting backstory as to why they were applying for the role, and where their respective careers had taken them. Two were semi-retired, others were simply freelance writers looking for their next job. Some had facial piercings, one had bright red hair, and two wore t-shirts to the interview. Some of this clearly challenged my assumptions about people and interviews. I decided that I would go with my gut and pull in the strongest candidates. I ultimately hired in five.

Leveling expectations

As the technical writing team onboarded, the first step was to determine what was needed to accomplish this, and so I met with the person responsible for overseeing this on the State's leadership team, let's call him Brandon. Brandon was a pleasant man, but deeply focused on the outcome, and would give a frank response to seemingly simple questions and assumptions. Understandably given the past failures, it was immediately apparent that Brandon had very specific expectations, and a process for how he wanted to be able to review the materials as they were devised, and a very specific mechanism for how these were to be delivered.

The fun part was aligning Brandon's expectations with the MSI's subject matter expert (let's call him Will) who was very much expecting to use the standard template (successfully implemented countless times in the past with clients), followed by team leads filling in the blanks, passing it over to the client, and calling it done. As you may have guessed, that wouldn't work in this case. Instead, I had to broker more than a couple of conversations to explain why and get these leaders together to hammer out what was going to be acceptable. Once all this was discussed in a few rounds of collaboration with Brandon and Will, I set to work mapping out the SMM in a spreadsheet and setting up preliminary meetings between myself and the SME leaders to explain the process. The entire schedule was mapped and printed on a conference wall 20 feet long and 10 feet high, and redone weekly, because it was such a critical deliverable.

Storming before performing

The five technical writers collocated together as a team and made their introductions to the ever-growing team of MSI SMEs. The stark contrast of suits and ties of the MSI office, along with the more casual appearance of the writing team started conversations flowing and raised more than just a few eyebrows. Stories of past experiences filled the air, and the stoic atmosphere was occasionally filled with an overabundance of laughter quickly followed by annoying glances from other teams. I remember thinking I'd made some critical errors in judgment bringing these groups together in one place. I learned very quickly that having the talent to hand is one thing, pulling it together and making it work is something quite different.

As I was managing my other deliverables, in addition to my other team, my hope was that the team would self-organize, so I left them to get acquainted with the task at hand and to discuss the approach. During this time, the security clearance for one of the technical writers was denied due to a minor misdemeanor more than a decade prior. The offence was completely unrelated to the job at hand, so I tried hard to justify why keeping this person made sense, but I ultimately had to let this person go. This of course meant the team was now down to four.

The writers and I met to discuss the approach. I laid out what was decided in terms of how we would build the documents, what the format would look like, and the expectations of the team. We discussed the SMM delivery board on the wall, and how we would use that to motivate the team leads to move forward with the documentation (to many, documentation was a last mile activity tacked onto an already challenging workload).

We needed to determine how to carve up the work and how to track it through the required approach Brandon had laid out. This included two separate reviews by the state SMEs, followed by editing rounds, and eventual approval. The team had very different ideas as to how we might accomplish this, and at least two different perspectives seemed to be competing. I set up individual meetings with each writer, and a weekly team meeting for an hour to discuss issues. To get into how we would deliver I suggested we hash it out over lunch.

Building cohesion

We went offsite for a working lunch for several hours, and it was clear the team appreciated going to a quality restaurant to work through our process together. Natural conversation flowed, but I could tell there was some tension. Once we had ordered, I gently nudged to discussing the problem at hand. I suggested the team use a Kanban board to track each document as it worked its way through the process and demonstrated how this might work. This would indicate who was working on which document at any given moment, keep a running history of who did what and when, and could leverage peer reviews for consistency. This seemed to resonate with the team. I suspect because creative types respond well with visual stimuli. One of the writers immediately connected with the concept and began mentally joining the dots from the Kanban workflows to the main schedule board that contained the dates we'd mapped out for each document. This person would clearly be my writing team lead, and in this moment the other team members began to see the value of how this person with a very big personality could step up. From this moment forward, the team began to gel.

The whole Kanban board was a series of large Post-It Notes that illustrated the work flows visually. The board on the wall kept the team focused on progress on the larger context of the SMM delivery and kept the MSI management abreast of progress simply by looking at the wall, without having to stop the work moving forward with more meetings.

Before long there was solid comradery, joined in a collective task that ebbed and flows between fun and challenging as reviews approached, and deadlines loomed. The writers, despite having a completely different professional background, gained credibility with the SME leads with their guidance and expertise in formatting and ultimately driving the documentation. Saving the SMEs countless hours of rework and ultimately making their lives easier. Despite differences in their respective personalities within the writing team, the common goal forged cohesion. Every few weeks I'd make the effort to repeat the lunch event, not so much to discuss work, but to keep the team spirit alive.

My team of technical writers, working among the SME leaders, delivered the SMM on time and to considerable appreciation from both the MSI and the State leaders. The sheer joy of creative mindsets truly made for a better workplace experience. In hindsight, this experience made me realize the power of diversity when we build teams. Melding different types of people has its challenges; we're human and each of us is unique and come from different cultures and perspectives. Individually each team member was mature, experienced, and capable of doing the work, some with unique quirks and personality traits, others very formal and focused.

My advice?

Just don't be afraid to blend worlds, it's what makes us human.

Note

1 https://www.linkedin.com/in/paul-thomason-1532781/

26 Why does it even matter?

OK, so you might buy in to the idea that project teams are different. You might agree that team dynamics are important to deliver success in an appropriate timeframe. And you may well understand the realities of scarce resources that have to be time managed to service many needs – both projects and business as usual.

But why does all that even matter?

To address this (possible) concern you might have let us consider some of the thought leaders views on this subject.

McKinsey's 'High-performing teams: A timeless leadership topic'[1] describes one team dynamic experience.

> *Team dynamics It's one thing to get the right team composition. But only when people start working together does the character of the team itself begin to be revealed, shaped by team dynamics that enable it to achieve either great things or, more commonly, mediocrity.*
>
> *Consider the 1992 roster of the US men's Olympic basketball team, which had some of the greatest players in the history of the sport, among them Charles Barkley, Larry Bird, Patrick Ewing, Magic Johnson, Michael Jordan, Karl Malone, and Scottie Pippen. Merely bringing together these players didn't guarantee success. During their first month of practice, indeed, the "Dream Team" lost to a group of college players by eight points in a scrimmage. "We didn't know how to play with each other," Scottie Pippen said after the defeat. They adjusted, and the rest is history. The team not only won the 1992 Olympic gold but also dominated the competition, scoring over 100 points in every game.*

Observation being that you can't magically put a team together and expect high-performance – it takes time.

Ernst and Young's article, 'How leaders can support team resilience and momentum'[2], describes the challenge of momentum.

DOI: 10.4324/9781003177753-26

> *Building team momentum. Achieving success as a team isn't easy, but maintaining that success is even more difficult. High-performing teams consistently achieve their goals when experiencing psychological momentum. Psychological momentum refers to the sensation teams experience when they feel like things are going from strength to strength, granting them a heightened sense of confidence, control, competence and self-belief.*

Observation being that high-performance requires constant focus.

Notes

1 https://www.mckinsey.com/business-functions/people-and-organizational-performance/our-insights/high-performing-teams-a-timeless-leadership-topic
2 https://www.ey.com/en_uk/workforce/how-leaders-can-support-team-resilience-and-momentum

27 The value of positive teams

In 'Positive Teams Are More Productive'[1] by Emma Seppälä it is noted that all managers would like their teams to be more productive (of course we would) but also observes that most companies are still using the same old methods (recognize that situation through a lot of my earlier consulting work).

> *Kim Cameron and his colleagues at the University of Michigan … have discovered a way to improve performance that has nothing to do with dishing out benefits or deploying new processes. In a research article published in the Journal of Applied Behavioural Science Cameron and his co-authors found that a workplace characterised by positive and virtuous practices excels in a number of domains.*
>
> *Positive and virtuous practices include:*
>
> - *Caring for, being interested in, and maintaining responsibility for colleagues as friends*
> - *Providing support for one another, including offering kindness and compassion when others are struggling*
> - *Avoiding blame and forgive mistakes*
> - *Inspiring one another at work*
> - *Emphasizing the meaningfulness of the work*
> - *Treating one another with respect, gratitude, trust & integrity*
>
> *Increase positive emotions which broaden employees' resources and abilities by improving people's relationships with each other and amplifying their creativity and ability to think creatively.*
>
> *Buffer against negative events like stress, improving employee's ability to bounce back from challenges and difficulties.*
>
> *Attract and bolster employees, making them more loyal and bringing out the best in them.*
>
> *There are bottom-line benefits as well. Summarizing the findings, Cameron explains that: "When organizations institute positive, virtuous practices they*

DOI: 10.4324/9781003177753-27

achieve significantly higher levels of organizational effectiveness—including financial performance, customer satisfaction, and productivity … The more the virtuousness, the higher the performance in profitability, productivity, customer satisfaction, and employee engagement.

I am a strong believer in building teams through the application of a 'fun' team spirit. In my book 'The Project Manager Who Smiled: The value of fun in project management[2]' I noted that:

Happy, positive people tend to live longer apparently:

A number of studies have shown that happy people tend to live longer. One study looked at a group of nuns who wrote a short biographical sketch before taking their vows. At the age of 85, 90% of the nuns with 'cheerful' biographies were still alive compared to 54% of the least 'cheerful'.

So be positive and you might make it to the end of that never-ending project.

Happy, positive people have the 'bounce back' factor:

It seems that happiness and an attitude of optimism tend to go hand in hand. Optimistic people see bad things as only temporary and good things as mostly permanent. Their positive expectation helps them see and act on opportunities faster and to overcome setbacks easier.

So be positive and you can deal with all of that [insert expletive of your choice here] that heads your way on the projects from hell[1].

Happy, positive people are better teamies:

There is also a strong link between feeling good and doing good. Studies have shown that happy people are more willing to help others, so happy people make the world a better place.

So be positive and your project team members will be all the better for it.

Happy, positive people feel pretty good about it all:

Let's face it, we all get a good feeling when we feel positive and upbeat, it is infectious isn't it? The better that we feel the more we achieve and get on with others and, as a direct result, we feel even more positive as a result.

Linked to that if we choose work that we like to do and that is meaningful to us, and that is challenging as well, it can generate those peak moments of enjoyment.

So be positive and enjoy your chosen profession of project management.

And, as I say in 'The Lazy Project Manager', the right sort of 'fun' project environment can be good for you as well, 'Done right you will have set the acceptable parameters for fun in your project, both in content and in extent, and you will have engendered that spirit amongst your project team to the point where, one day, when you are the one on a low, they will make come up and make you smile.

Notes

1 https://hbr.org/2015/03/positive-teams-are-more-productive
2 https://www.amazon.co.uk/project-manager-who-smiled-management/dp/0957668902

28 People first

All great stuff for sure but the reality is that you need to first move to a 'people first' focus and then gather the data intelligence to understand the people and aid/encourage/support/drive/lead a truly collaborative and trusting project team community.

To echo the wise words of Terry Cooke-Davies and Scott E. Patton in their PMI article 'Putting "people" at the center of project management[1]'

> *Projects are delivered by groups of people working together, and not by processes, project management tools, or clever project management systems. In many of the ways that matter as far as the management of projects is concerned, people and their behaviours haven't changed much. For all changes to our technological world, people still behave toward each other much as they have done since (at least) the dawn of recorded history. People are still moved to both helpful and unhelpful behaviours by their emotions (that is, after all, what the word e-motion implies–an impulse that leads to action), and projects, dealing as they do both with change and with temporary organizations, give rise to many such emotions.*

They continue with a reflection on the project leadership aspect of this.

> *Let us be controversial for a moment. Project and program managers themselves do not deliver their projects or programs. There is a sense in which they are a pure overhead cost. What they do, is manage the process, and the people who actually do the work to deliver the projects and programs. This work embraces both planning work and implementation work, as is well recognized in Bodies of Knowledge, but it is not PMs who do the work; they manage the people who do.*

Not controversial at all in my view (Figure 28.1).

The trajectory toward human engagement

> *The future of work was, of course, already on a trajectory towards greater flexibility and deeper human engagement; it has, however, just accelerated through several years-worth of progress in a few short months.*

DOI: 10.4324/9781003177753-28

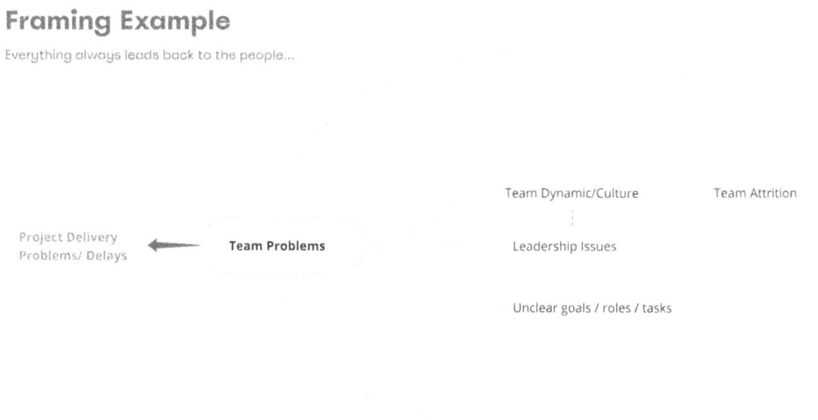

Figure 28.1 Framing example.

Deloitte[2] declared in the article 'Resilient Work – Transform work, the workforce, and the workplace'.

Projects are about people and yet 70% of our current effort goes on process.

Switching to a 'people first' approach.

What is missing from our understanding of project performance measurement?

For decades, project management executives and practitioners have been asking the multi-million, and sometimes multi-billion-dollar question, why did the project fail?

Whatever your definition may be for project success it is never an easy task getting there.

High project failure rates are nothing new and have been well documented. However, when project professionals seek answers to this question, they naturally turn back to the original project plan to identify flaws, be it the estimation, the requirements, or perhaps the business case. Yet there is one place where most don't look for the answers.

The people.

We know that throughout our project lifecycle there are a plethora of issues that can arise which can threaten the project success. These issues creep up on project managers despite the risk management performed and forecasts put in place, project leaders are constantly investigating where things went wrong analysing why they did and strategizing how they can be avoided in the future.

Of course, when these exercises are done the answers are not always found and if they ever are, it is all but too late. This breeds the need for a fresh approach to project performance, an approach which seeks to understand first and foremost, those that execute and receive the project plan, the people.

This approach should be a holistic one where all likelihoods are evaluated, and bias is removed, and it should be proactive and less reactive, less periodical, and more real time.

Nothing has actually changed

Not too long ago, I was at one of the major conferences in Europe, which was focused on PMOs. And during one of the breaks, after I completed my keynote presentation in the morning, I was talking to several people, as you do at these conferences – networking and all that.

One conversation I had was with one gentleman of a similar age to myself.

We were left alone at one of those coffee tables that you stand up at in conferences, and you know there's never enough room for drinks and food, etc., but we were talking to each other, and we reflected 'How was that we survived in the early days of being project managers, the time when we didn't even realise, we were project managers?'.

We reflected the fact that both of us had a remarkably similar sort of experience in that it was a number of years before we realized, we were acting as project managers, and it was several years before we were probably even called 'Project Managers', and certainly a number of years before we were given any form of education in being a project manager.

And yet somehow, in those early days, we survived.

The conclusion that we both came to was the fact that, whilst we did not understand what you might call the 'mechanics' of project management – the kind of hard process steps, the methodology, however you want to describe it – whilst we didn't understand that, because no one had taught us that, we were, therefore, by default, relying on the skills that we did have.

And these skills were predominantly people-oriented skills.

By focusing on the people, we were reasonably successful, moderately successful, sometimes a little unsuccessful I will be honest, but always learning important lessons. But the key thing was that we survived. We both survived in those early years, and it is because of that balance of capability of skills around people. We were pretty convinced that's the case anyway.

Now, certainly in later years, when we were both educated in the process, the method, the mechanics, or however you want to describe it, in project management it certainly helped us, it was certainly a huge benefit to understand the things that I had been doing okay and things I could certainly do better and some things I had not been doing at all. And it made me a better project manager.

But I think, on reflection, the industry and the profession has gone a little too far into the process side of things, and less into the area of the people. We have lost focus on the real 'success' element of projects.

Two aspects of this I am convinced that will drive us back to the 'people' are the topic of this book, projects, people, teams, performance, and that of the impact of AI (artificial intelligence) on the profession of project management.

In my book 'AI and the Project Manager: How the Rise of Artificial Intelligence Will Change Your World'[3] I recognize the opportunity to raise the focus on people through the application of AI.

> *… to take away the burdensome or the onerous tasks, to remove the stuff we don't really like doing, with some intelligence like AI could actually do better than us anyway. Never tiring, greater predictive capabilities, processing huge amounts of data, etc.*
>
> *It will allow us to free up our time, back to that 80% that Gartner[4] said will be released by AI. We will be able to spend our time interacting leading, and working with the people on our project team, wherever they are in the world. This is the quantum leap, this is the opportunity, that will allow the truth that projects are about people to become a reality.*
>
> *AI in project management will permit project managers, project leaders, change agents to spend time working with people to really get the best out of them.*

Notes

1 https://www.pmi.org/learning/library/putting-people-center-pm-6764
2 https://www2.deloitte.com/global/en/covid-19/resilient-work.html?id=uk:2ps:3gl:4resilience(resilienthub,_resilient_orgaization):GC1000014:6abt:20211001:gcp100039_3
3 AI and the Project Manager: How the Rise of Artificial Intelligence Will Change Your World https://www.amazon.co.uk/AI-Project-Manager-Artificial-Intelligence/dp/1032006579/ref=sr_1_1?crid=15K3VKNRFJOR4&keywords=ai+and+the+project+manager&qid=1648027005&sprefix=ai+and+the+proje%2Caps%2C104&sr=8-1
4 Gartner Says 80 Percent of Today's Project Management Tasks Will Be Eliminated by 2030 as Artificial Intelligence Takes Over https://www.gartner.com/en/newsroom/press-releases/2019-03-20-gartner-says-80-percent-of-today-s-project-management

29 The truth about project team performance

Project team performance is a supporting function of the achievement of objectives, goals, and (we hope) the business benefits described in the business case, all in the most efficient manner possible.

This efficiency is measured by the time taken to achieve these goals and the overall costs that will have been incurred during the project lifecycle.

Some example measures for such project team performance can include:

- Project success (objectives achieved)
- Quality of output
- Creativity levels
- Invested time consumed by phase or stage, and overall
- Financial usage
- Team member sentiment
- Engagement of team members
- Collaboration of team members
- Growth gain by each team member (career)

So, what can be done to increase the project team performance for your own projects?

In 'Project Team Performance – The missing piece to project success'[1] by my co-author, Bentzy,

> *To understand why projects fail, we often return to the project plan, the metrics used to measure success like budget and timelines, or whether there was a business need in the first place. But analysing these progress-related factors often fails to yield the answers we need. On the occasions we do get answers, they come too late to make the difference.*
>
> *While these process-related factors are important to consider, they can never give the full picture because they ignore one key piece of the puzzle: the people responsible for driving the project.*

DOI: 10.4324/9781003177753-29

> *Ultimately, projects are about people. It doesn't matter what project methodology you use, nor how well-conceived your plans are – if your team is not engaged and aligned, your project is doomed from the start.*

Obviously, I must totally concur with such thoughts, and it leads us to re-confirmation (if we needed it confirmed any more) that projects are about people and from there on to the realization that we also need data, people data, to get that focus on the people, and the teams.

The article goes on to declare

> *Time for a new approach. To ensure project success, we need a new approach to project management – one that seeks to understand and support the people responsible for delivering outcomes and executing plans. By focusing on people and empowering them to perform at their best, project success will naturally follow.*
>
> *Companies are quick to turn to quantitative data to predict the likelihood of project success. But data around tasks, timelines, and costs don't fully provide the insights you need to understand or predict project performance. We consider such data good for measuring project progress but not project performance.*
>
> *What's missing is another layer of data – one that until now has either been absent altogether or arrived too late to make a difference. We're talking, of course, about 'people data'.*

Note

1 https://www.linkedin.com/pulse/project-team-performance-missing-piece-success-bentzy goldman/

30 It is not big brother

Instead, it is gentle insights into team member feelings and state of motivation, or belief in the project objectives.

I like the idea of expected behaviours,[1] and example of which you can find in the Lisa A. DiTullio PMI article, when it comes to this aspect of project work.

> *The set of expected behaviours that have universal appeal to project teams are:*
>
> - *Treat others with dignity and respect*
> - *Support and promote intra- and inter-departmental teamwork*
> - *Understand and consider the needs and impacts of your own work on others*
> - *Demonstrate an ability to problem-solve and make timely decisions*
> - *Actively seek and receive feedback for improvement*
> - *Consistently share knowledge and information*
>
> *Introducing Expected Behaviors to project teams has a simple premise: Project work is conducted through groups; groups tend to be complex challenges from a management and communications point of view; if project teams come up with some ways to improve group dynamics, they can enhance group performance.*

All great thinking but, and this is the big one, how do you know?

How do I, as the project manager, working with, let's say a globally distributed project team really understand what the team are feeling, thinking, wanting, not wanting?

How do I know they are supporting the project goals still?

How do I know that they are supporting each other?

How do I know if we are in the performing, or the storming or the norming phase?

How do I know if they need help, more of my time?

How do I know if they want less of my time, and perhaps more of someone else's?

Without data – we simply don't. Yes, a project manager can do their very best to engage, listen, learn, gather feedback and more, but the bigger

DOI: 10.4324/9781003177753-30

the team, the more distributed the team, then the harder this becomes to gain any real-time appreciation of the sentiment of their project team.

We, the global community of project managers (and team leaders in general) need understanding.

And this requires insight.

And this requires data.

So, let's explore the data conundrum.

Note

1 https://www.pmi.org/learning/library/project-team-performance-expected-behaviors-6759

31 How is intelligence extracted from data?

It is best to start with a simple explanation of how 'data' becomes 'intelligence'.

I like the simple example provided in the Forbes article 'It's All About Data'[1] by Shankar Kambhampaty.

> *Data is text, audio, and video. For example, consider the data of the stocks listed on a stock exchange. If we were to add to that data the additional indicator of whether a particular stock moved up or down from the close of the previous day, it would become information—something that is of interest to us, and something we can analyse. When we add context to information, it becomes intelligence.*
>
> *If we were to look at the stock market data of 30 stocks representing a stock market index, that is just data. If we were to add the indicator that the stock market index in Singapore was down by 407 points at the close of business on a particular day but the Dow Jones was up by 330 points on that same day, then that is information. You can use that information to strive to predict how the market would open the following day in Singapore. That is intelligence.*

In my book 'Get Fit with The Lazy Project Manager: How to make sure your project is as healthy as possible and does not become the ex-project of tomorrow'[2] I speak to the data-information-knowledge-Wisdom model.

> *The DIKW Pyramid, also known variously as the 'DIKW Hierarchy' or 'Wisdom Hierarchy' refers loosely to one of a series of models for representing purported structural and/or functional relationships between data, information, knowledge, and wisdom.*
>
> - *Typically, information is defined in terms of data*
> - *Knowledge in terms of information*
> - *And wisdom in terms of knowledge*
>
> *In 1987, Czechoslovakia-born educator Milan Zeleny[3] mapped the elements of the hierarchy to these knowledge forms*

DOI: 10.4324/9781003177753-31

- *Know-nothing*
- *Know-what*
- *Know-how*
- *And know-why*

The 'DIKW' model proposes that data by itself has no meaning; it just fills databases and could, for example, be all the hours of effort recorded against a project, a big number probably but, in itself, meaningless.

Information arises when humans examine this data and provide a framework for understanding what the data represents. In this project I can see that 'x' hours were spent on this project task and 'y' on this task when both were expected to take 'z' hours.

Knowledge is the ability to take an action and it is created when information is used by individuals and organizations to devise a course of action and, often, this course of action is to generate more data thereby resulting in a new Data-Information-Knowledge cycle. In this project by assessing all of the time effort recorded we can see that there are variances that negatively impacted the schedule, if we compare this to another project using the same resources, we can identify like variances with some of those resources.

Wisdom encompasses the best and most appropriate action, and it usually results from multiple rounds of the Data-Information-Knowledge cycle. In our future projects we have learnt that if we use resource 'A' we would need to factor the effort estimates by '1.2' and for resource B by '1.3' in order to achieve the expected schedule results.

All about the data

But is not just about any old data, or in fact the data that we are used to have access to on our projects. The typical operational style data includes:

- Task
- Budget
- Timeline
- Resources

But what is needed in this new 'project team performance' centric world is more experiential data such as:

- Collaboration
- Autonomy
- Trust
- Purpose

This is what will drive insights and intelligence (wisdom eventually) for project managers in the future.

Data to find the customer

The concept of reversing the normality of business data is one that fascinates and excites me.

In the past it has always been a case of business leaders reaching out to view the data that is made available to them through various business intelligence platforms, but it was, mostly, a pull situation. I need to know 'A' and so I secure a report, or a BI status output and I assess the situation, in the moment, and then make a decision.

But, in this world of data insights, it is a matter of an individual wanting to know the answer to a specially defined question, at that specific point.

The concept of the 'data finding the customer' is a switch of this process. One where the business or project leader is automatically supplied the data on a need to know (and need to know right now) basis. It is a push supply of intelligence, supported by advisory action guidance.

As a project manager to gain insights such as this, in the understanding of the dynamics and sentiment of my project team members, in real-time, and based on honest inputs, would be enormously valuable.

Think of it this way. I have a nice new car that is packed full of lasers and sensors and all manner of digital tracking devices, and it constantly monitors my driving. Drift across a line in the road and it gently (at least to begin with) helps correct my direction. Drive too fast and/or too close to another vehicle and it offers an audible warning before, if I ignore it completely, bringing the vehicle rapidly to a halt (I have experienced this only once and it was both impressive and sudden). All the time the car (or its electronic brain) is deciding what, by exception, it advises me, and what, by even more exception, it needs to intercede and correct.

Imagine on a project that similar data tracking is taking place, gathering small 'insights', often and easily to validate the 'pulse' of the project team, and therefore the project itself.

Moving away from the lagging project indicators to a world of proactive analytics on what is likely to happen, rather than what has happened and what can we do about it now?

This is the world of the continuous pulse and the truly proactive approach.

In the words of my co-author, Bentzy,

> *say goodbye to surprises in your teams. Know what's coming before it affects team dynamics and productivity.*

Notes

1 https://www.forbes.com/sites/forbestechcouncil/2018/07/23/its-all-about-data/
2 https://www.amazon.co.uk/Get-Fit-Lazy-Project-Manager-ebook/dp/B00PG9DS54
3 Milan Zeleny is a Czech American economist, currently a Professor of Management Systems at Fordham University, New York City. He has done research in the field of decision-making, productivity, knowledge management, and business economics.

32 Project intelligence

There are probably as many definitions of intelligence as there are experts who study it. Simply put, however, intelligence can be described as the ability to learn about, learn from, understand, and interact with one's environment.

'It's not that I'm so smart, it's just that I stay with problems longer.' – Albert Einstein[1]

This general ability consists of several specific abilities including:

- Adaptability to a new environment or to changes in the current environment
- Capacity for knowledge and the ability to acquire it
- Capacity for reason and abstract thought
- Ability to comprehend relationships
- Ability to evaluate and judge
- Capacity for original and productive thought

Environment in this definition has a wider meaning that includes a person's immediate surroundings, including the people around him or her. Environment in this case can also be something as small as a family, the workplace, or perhaps a project team.

A project, as we all know, is a temporary endeavor, having a defined beginning and end (usually constrained by date, but can be by funding or deliverables, undertaken to meet unique goals and objectives, and usually to bring about beneficial change or added value. The temporary nature of projects stands in contrast to business as usual (or operations), which are repetitive, permanent, or semi-permanent functional work to produce products or services.

But what if you combine 'intelligence' with 'projects', what would you achieve?

Well, a successful project manager certainly needs to address the specific intelligence abilities:

DOI: 10.4324/9781003177753-32

- Adaptability to a new environment or to changes in the current environment – projects are all about delivering change and the ability to oversee such change requires a great degree of adaptability.
- Capacity for knowledge and the ability to acquire it – projects also require a continuous learning process to understand the change that is being delivered, the lessons that are there to be learned. The combined knowledge of the core and extended project team offer the best platform for project success.
- Capacity for reason and abstract thought – logical application through the methods of project management will deliver a degree of likely success, the ability to 'think outside the box' and supply beneficial adaptations to process and solutions will deliver the rest.
- Ability to comprehend relationships – projects are all about people and the relationship of people with other people.
- Ability to evaluate and judge – such is the essence of project leadership and decision-making.
- Capacity for original and productive thought – problem resolution and the comparative analysis of options is a constant need in good project management.

So, in all aspects the project demands the intelligent project manager.

But what else is required to support successful project delivery, not from the individual's perspective but from the organization as a whole?

Here we can introduce a new term that refers to these requirements, Project Intelligence.

Project Intelligence refers to the skills, processes, technologies, applications, metrics, and practices used to support successful project delivery from the organisation.

Common components of Project Intelligence include:

- Project Management skills, maturity, and certification (from project contributor through to senior project (or program) roles)
- Project Methodologies and practices
- Project Management Information Systems
- Project (or Program) Management Office (PMO) activities and focus (supportive, directive, controlling)
- Executive/Management skills, maturity, and experience in project delivery
- Project-based organizational maturity
- Project Support technologies (Resource Management, Skills Database, Scheduling and Time Management, Invoicing or Cost Management)
- Project Dashboard and Reporting technologies

Project Intelligence aims to support a project-based organizations' successful project capability.

Project Intelligence is all about having the very best environment to nurture and deliver project success through the needed skills, processes, technologies, applications, metrics, and practices.

But, since we have observed, intelligence can be described as the ability to learn about, learn from, understand, and interact with one's environment, the problem then is of time.

Project managers, and project teams are busy, under pressure, driven by time and cost and quality and scope constraints. The bigger the project team the harder it is for any project manager to truly 'know' how their team members are feeling, and that is a big problem.

Such project intelligence, insight as it were, I strongly believe, offers project managers the opportunity to gain the very best out of the people on the team, both as individuals and as a collective.

Therefore, the number one focus that all project-based organizations need to invest both time and money in is … fanfare … people-focused project intelligence.

Projects are (yes, I am saying one more time) about people.

Period.

Note

1 "The Ultimate Quotable Einstein," edited by Alice Calaprice (Princeton University Press, 2011).

33 Part 3: Futures

In Part 3 Bentzy Goldman and Peter Taylor bring forward a final argument that high performing teams should be continually examining their interpersonal dynamics and collective approach to challenges, and that a focus on project team performance will be the next quantum leap in project success.

It is all about putting people back into project management, and to putting a people focus back into team dynamics.

DOI: 10.4324/9781003177753-33

34 Old way – new way thinking

Bentzy: I took us on a journey to look into the future of work itself, exploring the purpose and values of teams, the increase in the project culture in work that underpins much of what we 'do' at work each day.

I tried to provide some insight into what makes a team a high-performance team, which included the concept of servant leadership and a people-first approach.

And finally, I considered the intelligence of team analytics to power the team performance aspirations that all forward-thinking and smart working organisations are aspiring to.

Peter: And to follow on from that opening exploration, I posed the challenge that projects are just different, at least different when it comes to people and to team behaviour.

I then argued for the understanding of the 'Disrupting' aspect to project team dynamics and considered the massive growth in pure virtual and hybrid team working patterns.

Finally concluding with the realization that project leaders, sponsors (and team members) need some help around project intelligence to benefit from the 'projects are about people' reality.

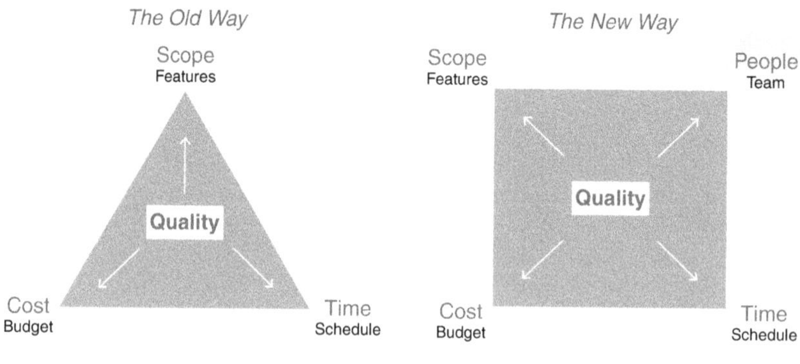

Figure 34.1 PremoteMe Inc – The old way – the new way.

DOI: 10.4324/9781003177753-34

35 T.E.A.M

The motto of one of the authors own Global PMO is simple, it is 'Together Everyone Achieves More'[1] and, in the unlikely event of you not also believing this Bentzy laid out some compelling arguments for this not being the case:

- Teams allow for division of labour: each person can focus on their strengths and the team can get more done in less time.
- Teams lead to more creativity and collaboration: teams can bounce ideas off each other and come up with creative solutions to problems.
- Teams provide support and encouragement to each other, leading to a higher engaged and productive workforce.

And he further declared that there was a real 'power' to teams, in that they are more likely to achieve larger goals than individuals alone, they are more likely to be innovative, more productive, and more adaptive as changes in the marketplace or workplace occur.

The advantages of teams over individual workers seem to be very clear.

But Peter noted that the challenge today, and increasingly so into the future, is that projects are becoming ever more complex in their nature, with increased expectations of delivery, and greater scale. That teams are becoming more 're-mote' in nature all of which, adds to the challenge of team leaders to know how their team members are feeling and what they can do to aid performance levels and engagement and aligned ambition for the purpose of their collective work.

This is, effectively, a final argument that high-performing teams should be continually examining their interpersonal dynamics and collective approach to challenges, and that a focus on project team performance will be the next quantum leap in project success.

But how can you take advantage if this 'people' and 'team' centric future in your own organization?

Note

1 There is an alternative version that is Together Everyone Annoys Me, but honestly, people who think this way are in the minority we feel.

DOI: 10.4324/9781003177753-35

36 But this is an HR thing

So have many said to us ... But the thing is, we would have called the book 'new tools and thinking for HR' if these ideas were meant for them – It was written for team and project leaders intentionally. Many times, when we speak to business and specifically project leaders, they say 'why are you coming to me if this is a people tool, go to HR'. I yawn and go on to explain that, as Peter so clearly outlined, 'everything goes back to the people' – people deliver projects.

It was a shock to me when I initially learned that this was common practice – measuring and empowering teams to continuously improve (outside of just the work task).

Yes, in most companies, performance and engagement are the domains of HR. They collect data through centralized, bureaucratic processes, using tools such as performance reviews and employee engagement surveys. These processes require a lot of time and effort to set up and roll out, and, in our fast-paced world of work, their value for managers and teams is questionable. For executives, it is crucial to grasp what's going on in their organizations and to understand why people might feel disengaged or decide to resign. But these insights are often slow to make their way to management, and it's certainly too late to make any immediate use of the information during a project by the time it comes to light. Team members that leave projects and potentially derail its probability of success – has nothing to do with HR, and everything to do with their team, management, and the project at hand.

Leaving it to HR alone is not only counterproductive, but also a way to alleviate the accountability and responsibility for ensuring that team members are satisfied in their work and team.

DOI: 10.4324/9781003177753-36

37 The Goldman-Taylor five principles of progression

The following are the five principles that are first required to be acknowledged and then utilized as the building block for your own progression to a future world of high-performing teams driven by great people leadership – powered through team analytics.

1 Acceptance that it's time for a new approach

One cannot go about making a change effectively if they don't believe that change is necessary. The first step to progress is to accept the necessity for progress to be made.

Really understanding the importance of a people-centric approach, and that people-related insight should be far more readily accessible to managers and their teams, and that they should be delivered much faster. After all, these are the people who work on the front lines every day; those who can make an immediate difference to an organization's performance. They can do this by starting with *team* performance and *team* well-being to ultimately achieve *team* success.

Empowering managers and their teams to set up and access their own team-generated insights is crucial for them to be able to make strategic decisions to tackle issues as they arise, and not after they blow up. If a manager's team is out of sync, they need to know *now* – not next week or the end of the quarter. Without timely insights, managers are essentially left flying blind, unable to understand the human factors that impact team dynamics, performance, and engagement.

2 Empowering managers has never been more important

The world is changing at an increasingly fast pace. Because the pandemic has accelerated the transition to remote work and in-person interactions (both formal and informal) have fallen by the wayside, it has never been more important for managers to find ways to keep their fingers on the pulse regarding their teams' performance and engagement. Working virtually will

DOI: 10.4324/9781003177753-37

inevitably make issues harder to notice and will increase the likelihood of problems sneaking up on unsuspecting managers.

As the rate of change accelerates, organizations must become more agile. Those who can adapt rapidly will survive; those who aren't, won't. To make the right decisions swiftly, managers need data delivered in real-time. They need *leading* data points on team performance that can help them tackle issues as they arise – not *lagging* data points that highlight issues after they've come to the fore – measuring performance not merely to *evaluate* team members but to *empower* them.

> 'We cannot solve our problems with the same thinking we used when we created them'.
>
> Albert Einstein[1]

3 This change is critical for all project-based teams

As we've stated – The need for real-time performance data is particularly pressing for managers of project-based teams. The way these cross-functional teams operate and the way they are assembled and disassembled means that they face greater uncertainty and urgency than functional teams do. As a result, a great deal of agility is required from project-based teams.

To succeed consistently in our projects, we have to give managers and teams the insights they need to solve problems collectively, before they escalate, and to make more informed decisions. This need will only become more apparent with the ongoing shift toward project teams and away from traditional teams in our world of work.

4 Identifying areas for improvement

In some way, many organizations are doing some form of team feedback, retrospection, or assessment already, albeit ineffectively. It is generally too infrequent, not mandated, systematic or automated – but there it's a great way to start by identifying the closest thing to what you already have and expand on that as a low-hanging fruit. Retrospectives are unfortunately mostly focused on work and not the team, they're not always inclusive – often having the same team members always contributing their opinions, with the quieter bunch staying silent.

Most people don't really anticipate retros with excitement. We've seen many teams start by improving their retro practice by implementing our tool and then rocking up to a retro equipped with insights and ready to act together as a team – often already having asynchronously found solutions. This also allows all team members to participate and provide suggestions without feeling any form of trepidation or fear of scrutinization. We spoke about team assessments, consultants coming in, and the different types of health checks that management does – these are also great options to take advantage of for implementing Perflo as an improvement and eventual replacement.

5 Start today, not tomorrow

The authors truly hope that, through reading this book, and through other research and experience, you will have reached the (inevitable) conclusion that this change is coming.

As such the 'call to action' is simply 'start today', don't leave it to see what happens to other organizations, or what happens to other teams, instead take the lead, take control, take advantage. Today!

As noted in principle #4, you are, most likely, already doing this in some way and this can form the platform for progression to a much more productive world of Team Analytics, which we believe is the future of high-performance teams and project success.

Note

1 "The Ultimate Quotable Einstein," edited by Alice Calaprice (Princeton University Press, 2011).

38 Part 4: Roadmap

In Part 4 Bentzy Goldman and Peter Taylor consider an appropriate 'roadmap' for you to follow to reach the future of high-performance teams and project success based on the lessons shared, the insights and the future considerations detailed in this book.

DOI: 10.4324/9781003177753-38

39 How to go about the transformation

What we've seen to be successful in this shift of process (and sometimes mindset) is to first and foremost identify one or more champions who are passionate about the problem, the solution, and have the influence to create change and influence others in the organization. Naturally this would be a people-centric manager or leader who understands the value and doesn't need convincing of why it's important to prioritize people in projects.

We have seen head of agile/transformation in larger companies, heads of PMOs, or senior scrum masters, agile coaches or program managers take charge as well.

Bottom-up vs top-down.

We're all aware of the different avenues to go when it comes to process or software implementation. Dependent on what you are implementing and, of course, factors such as company size, culture, and process – there are certain advantages and disadvantages of opting for either avenue, however when it comes to a behavior change there are two crucial things to get right in the implementation process no matter which avenue you take (of course it is ideal for managers to have some level of autonomy to select safe tools that will help them and their teams be more productive and healthy):

Team buy-in

We are putting this one as the top priority, and we'll explain why.

Without the team's buy-in, the process and tool you chose are destined to fail.

Teams need to understand the value, the why and most importantly 'how will it benefit us?' prior to any actual use or piloting of a solution or process. If all of those are not clearly understood and accepted as valid by team members – you're entering an uphill battle of reminders, frustration, and cost efficiency. It goes without saying that before the team understands the need and importance – managers need to first.

DOI: 10.4324/9781003177753-39

Manager accountability

If managers are not accountable for implementing and using this new process or tool, how do we expect their teams to be committed.

We are not advocates for any type of fear-based motivation, however, in this instance, their ought to be some consequence for managers who are essentially ignoring their team's needs on a continuous basis.

Forget new process or new tool – we are trying to better understand team needs much quicker and more efficiently. The goal being to help support them, increase team efficiency, and project success. If these outcomes are not in the best interest of managers, well they shouldn't be there in the first place. If they are, they need to change their ways and recognize the importance, or rather necessity of modern leadership styles. A team's satisfaction levels and productivity combined will naturally expose the leadership style of its leader, so it shouldn't take a new process like this to expose them – but if that is the case – the necessary action should be self-explanatory, provided that Learning and Development have already tried the leading the horse to water approach.

Sponsorship

Let's be realistic here, all change in business demands that there is the right level of sponsorship in place otherwise, typically, ideas and initiatives wither and die quite quickly.

Sponsor(s) should guide the change leaders, ensure that all important management accountability is effectively in place, and support the logical acquisition of the right level of external and objective experience to work with their business leaders to bring about successful transformation.

Learning and sharing lessons

The key here is that you need to both 'learn' and then effectively, 'shares' lessons learned.

The former without the latter is pointless.

These insights are essential for understanding of what happened and where improvements can be made in the future, and for how we may run current and future projects more effectively.

40 Gaining the team buy-in

As was noted, this one is the top priority because without the team's buy-in, the process and tool you chose are destined to fail. It is interesting that all digital transformation is really about the people first.

But consider these tips for positioning the new process/tool to your team

- Emphasize it is a tool for the team and not for managers
- Clarify that no data will be used for individual performance/HR or penalization
- Reinforce they are partners for the success of this new tool
- Explain how it will benefit them directly by improving the overall team experience, productivity, and getting the support that they need
- Then show how it fits into the organization's goals and purpose (Figure 40.1).

Addressing the 'WHY'

Have a conversation with your team:

'What we want to get out of this?'

For example – Together with you, we want to …

- Run more effective and contextual meetings and check-ins
- Understand our team better and how we can support them
- Detect potential project or people issues early on and act
- Have a centralized place to give feedback and suggestions
- Track team alignment and team sentiment
- Identify areas for leadership improvements
- Ensure the right people are on the right projects (which they enjoy)

Bonus tips

- Figure out who the promoters are and use them as champions to drive engagement

DOI: 10.4324/9781003177753-40

Team-Buy in Tips

HIGH LEVEL	TEAM LEVEL
• Help you feel included in project planning/tracking/ decision making.	• Have more clarity about the purpose, roles and expectations at the start of projects.
• Have a platform to provide feedback and suggestions.	• Ensure you have the resources needed to do your work successfully.
• Take relevant action that has direct impact on project and team success.	• Ensure teammates are being held accountable and the team is collaborating in a healthy way.
• Have a record of the team's perspective throughout their time together.	• Ensure you have the support you need from your team lead and organization.
• Have insight on how the team could be managed or supported better.	• Monitor your workload and stress levels to ensure healthy and balanced working environments.
• Eventually match the team with work they are excited about.	• Ensure your team lead is actively leading the team in an effective and positive way.

Figure 40.1 Team buy-in tips.

- See who is resisting to the tool and ask why – try to understand the root cause
- Always recognize and praise the team's participation and commitment
- Always close the loop to ensure that team buy-in is gaining traction

41 Dealing with manager accountability

It is a matter of a critical partnership since if managers are not accountable for implementing and using this new process or tool, then how can anyone possibly expect their teams to be equally committed.

But beware of the manager paradox – good vs bad managers.

The irony when approaching these types of tools and processes is – good managers need it less but are quicker to adopt (and sometimes tend to have some process in place already which can be improved upon), and bad managers need it more but don't care enough to implement, or possibly go out of their way to avoid implementation.

The same goes for organizations.

People-centric companies with positive work cultures tend to not need the education piece, and the more traditional organizations that are not yet fully people-centric, have a stronger need for change but are also the ones who are more resistant to it.

We've seen this also with organizations who've adopted an agile approach (team analytics aligns with their principles and desire for continuous improvement). Something we came to realize was that the organizations wanting to adopt agile could use this change as a great way to drive and measure adoption of agile across all their teams!

Nevertheless, it is important not to influence managers with a fear-based approach. Yes, the health of their teams should be incorporated into their rewards plan, but that is a reward, not a threat.

There's nothing more satisfying to watch when we see that teams and managers become aligned, communicate better, and increase their performance and general well-being, by adopting these practices!

DOI: 10.4324/9781003177753-41

42 Securing the all-important sponsorship

Everyone knows that any business change demands the right level of sponsorship to be in place, otherwise even the most passionate employee led initiative is more than likely to wither and die very swiftly.

There are perhaps two critical keys to gaining this executive sponsorship for the new team-centric world. It is always a matter of 'what's in it for the business', and 'what's in it for them'.

- Show how the business and the sponsor will benefit from the change in approach
    - Perhaps this book will help, certainly the ideas and arguments within should add to your argument
    - Look at other research into this area and the value of team analytics
    - Consider what other businesses are doing, competitors or otherwise
    - Introduce experts from outside of the business to present, discuss, and 'sell' the new way
- Demonstrate a commitment to change
    - Yourself, your teams, your peers, and your colleagues, all aligning to support the change in approach – offer up your time and focus on leading or piloting this business change
    - Passion in yourself will instill passion on others

DOI: 10.4324/9781003177753-42

43 Steps to success

1. Define what you want to know and why (management)
2. Get team input for potential areas to measure or what has been an issue previously
3. Keep the conversations and plans transparent and encourage contribution
4. Ensure alignment across senior and lower management as well as team members
5. Pilot the process and tool in a few teams first to learn and improve on the implementation
6. Continuously review the feedback and learn what the team needs
7. Brainstorm and take action to address those target areas

DOI: 10.4324/9781003177753-43

44 A helping hand

And yes, getting some help is not a demonstration of weakness but rather the wise step of any organization to rapidly secure understanding and guidance in approaching such a critical change in process, mindset, and focus.

DOI: 10.4324/9781003177753-44

45 Team analytics: The future of high-performance teams and project success

Peter and Bentzy hope that this book has inspired you and encouraged you to start your journey to a new 'people'-oriented future and wish you, and your organization, all the best for this exciting journey ahead.

This book aimed to explore a new approach to project success, the continuous process of enabling and empowering teams to reach the optimal levels of performance, and we hope that we have inspired you in some small way to embrace this new future.

We are here to give you that helping hand if you need us.

Good luck!

> *Great things in business are never done by one person. They're done by a team of people. Steve Jobs*[1]

> *The way a team plays as a whole determines its success. You may have the greatest bunch of individual stars in the world, but if they don't play together, the club won't be worth a dime. Babe Ruth*[2]

Notes

1 https://www.businessnewsdaily.com/4195-business-profile-steve-jobs.html
2 https://quotefancy.com/babe-ruth-quotes

DOI: 10.4324/9781003177753-45

Appendices

Authors

Bentzy Goldman

Figure 46.1 Bentzy Goldman.

Bentzy is the founder of Perflo, an innovative technology start-up that helps teams and their organizations to measure and increase performance using cutting-edge research in team psychology.

He is extremely passionate about and speaks on topics related to the future of work – dreaming of a world where Monday mornings are looked forward to, not resented.

www.perflo.co – Team Analytics.

Perflo is a team diagnostics solution that empowers managers via smart nudges to lead teams proactively, while generating actionable insights for organizations to increase team efficiency and well-being.

Peter Taylor

Keynote speaker and coach, Peter is the author of the number 1 bestselling project management book 'The Lazy Project Manager', along with many other books on Project Management, PMO development, Executive Sponsorship, Transformation Leadership, and Speaking Skills.

Figure 46.2 Peter Taylor.

He has built and led some of the largest PMOs in the world with organizations such as Siemens, IBM, UKG, and now Ceridian, where he is the VP Global PMO.

He has also delivered over 500 lectures around the world in 25 countries and has been described as 'perhaps the most entertaining and inspiring speaker in the project management world today'.[1]

You can discover more about Peter through his website www.thelazyprojectmanager.com and also through his podcast, The Squid of Despair,[2] at www.squidofdespair.com

Other Routledge publications:

- Project Management: It's All Bollocks
- Make Your Business Agile: A Roadmap for Transforming Your Management and Adapting to the 'New Normal'
- AI and the Project Manager: How the Rise of Artificial Intelligence Will Change Your World

Notes

1 To be clear, this was not a quote from his mother.

2 With his co-host, David Ayling-Smith (Unscripted podcast musings on business life, leadership, creativity, transformation, and all the myriad of other work-life events that get in the way of a good night's sleep).

Index

agile coach 105
AI 50–51, 85
Albinson, Damion 69
alignment 20
Amazon 93
Ariely, Dan 16
Aristotle 57, 58
Ashkenas, Ron 56
autonomy 20
Ayling-Smith, David 115

Belbin 59, 64
Biggs, Timothy 62
Bion, Wilfred 59

Cameron, Kim 79
Campbell, Billy 28
Claprice, Alice 96
clarity 25, 45–46
cognitive diversity 9
continuous improvement 24, 69
continuous learning 20
Cooke-Davies, Terry 82
Covid-19 6

Deloitte 7, 69, 72, 83
Deloitte Dec-13
demographic diversity 9
DIKW 90–91
Dilbert 71
DISC 64
DiTullio, Lisa 88
Dow Jones 90

Einstein, Albert 94, 96, 102–103
empathetic leadership 20
Ernst and Young 77
experiential diversity 9

Ferguson, Alex 27
Forbes 7
Forbes 7, 90, 93

Galton, Francis 29
Garret, Dave xi
Gartner 85
Gen-Z 14–17, 19, 38
Getty, J. Paul 17
Glassdoor 14
Goldman, Bentzy 114
Goldman-Taylor 101–103
growth mindset 27

Harvard 49
Harvard Business Review 56
Hawthorne studies 6
health check 33
human-centric organization 14
humor 18
hybrid working 98

IBM 52
information sharing 22

Jobs, Steve 113

Kambhampathy, Shankar 90
Kanban 76
Klopp, Jurgen 27

lessons learned 106
Lewin, Kurt 59, 63

machine learning 53
Marston, William Moulton 64
Matta, Nadim 56
McKinsey 9, 37, 49, 77

micro-assessment 34
Microsoft 40
MIT 64
Moger, Susan 63–64
multi-source integrator 73
mutual respect 20
Myers Briggs 59

NASA 12
natural language processing 51
New Hay Group 49
NLP 51
nudges 47–48

Patton, Scott E. 82
Perflo 33–35, 38, 103
PMI 69, 82, 88
PMO 73, 84, 95, 99, 105
PreMoteMe 98
Project Aristotle 49
project intelligence 95–96
psychological safety 20, 26, 39
PwC 12

radical candour 26
Randstat 10
retrospectives 102
Rickards, Tudor 63–64
Routledge 52, 57
Ruth, Babe 113

Salas 12
Salesforce 16
Schutz 59
scrum master 105
Seddon, Richard 69
Seppala, Emma 79
servant leadership 23, 52
Slack 40
SMM 74–75
social cohesiveness 21
sponsorship 106
Stein, Judith 59
stress 44–45
success 111
super team Dec-13
Surowiecki, James 31

Taylor, Peter 114
team analytics 41–43
team buy-in 107–108
team cohesion 25
team islands 59, 64
team retrospection 26
team science 13
team trust 21
team-centric 110
Teams 40
The Lazy Project Manager 55, 81
Thomason, Paul 73–76
Thomson 7
trust 25
Tuckman, Bruce 59–64, 66–68, 70, 72

Unilever 17

virtual team performance 21

wisdom hierarchy 90
work-life balance 27
Wrike 57

Zeleny, Milan 90, 93

For Product Safety Concerns and Information please contact our EU
representative GPSR@taylorandfrancis.com
Taylor & Francis Verlag GmbH, Kaufingerstraße 24, 80331 München, Germany

www.ingramcontent.com/pod-product-compliance
Ingram Content Group UK Ltd.
Pitfield, Milton Keynes, MK11 3LW, UK
UKHW022313250926
475702UK00046B/768
9781032012230